150

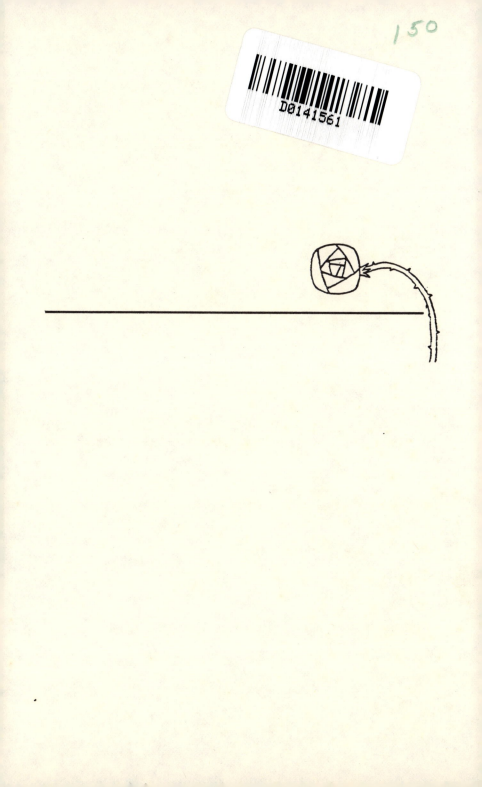

CHRISTIANITY PATRIARCHY and ABUSE

A Feminist Critique

Edited by
Joanne Carlson Brown
Carole R. Bohn

The Pilgrim Press   New York

Second printing, 1990

Biblical quotations, unless otherwise noted, are from the Revised Standard Version of the Bible, copyright 1946, 1952, © 1971, 1973 by the Division of Christian Education of the National Council of the Churches of Christ in the U.S.A., and are used by permission.

Royalties from the sale of this volume will be given to the Center for Prevention of Sexual and Domestic Violence, 1914 N. 34 St., Seattle, Washington 98103.

Library of Congress Cataloging-in-Publication Data

Christianity, patriarchy, and abuse : a feminist critique / edited by
Joanne Carlson Brown and Carole R. Bohn.
          p. cm.
        ISBN 0-8298-0808-6
      1. Violence—Religious aspects—Christianity. 2. Patriarchy—
Religious aspects—Christianity. 3. Feminism—Religious aspects—
Christianity. I. Brown, Joanne Carlson. II. Bohn, Carole R.
                      BT736.15.C465   1989
    261.8′3—dc20   89-35505

The Pilgrim Press, 475 Riverside Drive, New York, NY 10115

Contents

Contributors   vii

Foreword   xi
    ELIZABETH BETTENHAUSEN

INTRODUCTION   xiii

1. For God So Loved the World?   1
    JOANNE CARLSON BROWN and REBECCA PARKER

2. The Western Religious Tradition and Violence Against
    Women in the Home   31
    ROSEMARY RADFORD RUETHER

3. And a Little Child Will Lead Us: Christology and Child
    Abuse   42
    RITA NAKASHIMA BROCK

4. Sexual Violence: Patriarchy's Offense and Defense   62
    KAREN L. BLOOMQUIST

5. Christian "Virtues" and Recovery from Child Sexual
    Abuse   70
    SHEILA A. REDMOND

Contents

6. Theological Pornography: From Corporate to Communal
   Ethics   89
   MARY HUNT

7. Dominion to Rule: The Roots and Consequences of a
   Theology of Ownership   105
   CAROLE R. BOHN

8. The Fallacy of Individualism and Reasonable Violence
   Against Women   117
   POLLY YOUNG-EISENDRATH and DEMARIS WEHR

9. The Transformation of Suffering: A Biblical and
   Theological Perspective   139
   MARIE F. FORTUNE

10. Pain and Pleasure: Avoiding the Confusions of Christian
    Tradition in Feminist Theory   148
    BEVERLY W. HARRISON and CARTER HEYWARD

Contributors

Elizabeth Bettenhausen
  Walker Ecumenical Exchange
  Newton, Massachusetts

Karen L. Bloomquist
  Church and Society Staff
  Evangelical Lutheran Church in America

Carole R. Bohn
  Assistant Professor of Pastoral Psychology
  Boston University

Rita Nakashima Brock
  Assistant Professor of Religion
  Pacific Lutheran University

Joanne Carlson Brown
  Professor of Church History and Ecumenics
  St. Andrews College, Canada

Marie F. Fortune
  Director, Center for Prevention of Sexual and Domestic Violence
  Seattle, Washington

Contributors

Beverly W. Harrison
 Professor of Christian Social Ethics
 Union Theological Seminary, New York

Carter Heyward
 Associate Professor of Theology
 Episcopal Divinity School

Mary Hunt
 Director, Women's Alliance for Theology, Ethics, and Ritual
 Silver Spring, Maryland

Rebecca Parker
 President, Starr King School for the Ministry
 Berkeley, California

Sheila A. Redmond
 Ph.D. Candidate
 University of Ottawa

Rosemary Radford Ruether
 Georgia Harkness Professor of Applied Theology
 Garrett Evangelical Theological School

Demaris Wehr
 Adjunct Faculty
 Episcopal Divinity School

Polly Young-Eisendrath
 Lecturer in Human Development
 Bryn Mawr College

CHRISTIANITY
PATRIARCHY
and
ABUSE

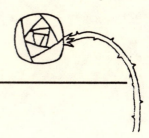

Foreword

ELIZABETH BETTENHAUSEN

The line between violence and awe is a deadly blur in popular culture in the United States. The first test explosion of a nuclear bomb in the desert of New Mexico in 1945 led J. Robert Oppenheimer to recall John Donne's poem, "Batter my heart, three-person'd God." The success of this deadliest force required a theology in which being faithful is the equivalent of being conquered and raped by divine power. Here, religion, sexuality, and violence became intertwined in a way few dare to examine. The contributors to this volume have that courage.

Several years ago I asked a group of seminarians to choose New Testament stories about Jesus and rewrite them imagining that Jesus had been female. The following re-creation of the passion story of Luke 22:54–65 was one woman's knowing by the heart.

They arrested the Christ woman and led her away to the Council for questioning. Some of her followers straggled along to find out what was to become of her. There were seven women and two men followers. (The men followers were there mainly to keep watch over their sisters.) Someone from among the crowd asked a question of a man follower, "Haven't I seen you with this woman? Who is she, and what is your relationship with her?" He replied defensively, "She is a prostitute, she has had many men. I have seen her with many!"

The men who were guarding the Christ slapped her around and made fun of her. They told her to use magic powers to stop them. They blindfolded her and each of them in turn raped her and afterward jeered,

"Now, prophetess, who was in you? Which one of us? Tell us that!" They continued to insult her. (Kandice Joyce)

After this story was read aloud, a silence surrounded the class and made us shiver. Ever since, I have wondered, Would women ever imagine forming a religion around the rape of a woman? Would we ever construe gang-rape as a salvific event for other women? What sort of a god would such an event reveal?

As several of the following essays recount, Christian theology has long imposed upon women a norm of imitative self-sacrifice based on the crucifixion of Jesus of Nazareth. Powerlessness is equated with faithfulness. When the cross is also interpreted as the salvific work of an all-powerful paternal deity, women's well-being is as secure as that of a child cowering before an abusive father. Theological revolution is made all the more urgent by the daily suffering that theological metaphors of redemptive violence only encourage.

At the same time, a theological interpretation of suffering is essential. Until suffering is eliminated, its agony is fed when no sense can be made of it. But how can we give meaning to suffering without sanctioning it? Can a theology be developed that holds that no violence or suffering, including the violent death of Jesus of Nazareth, is ever divine will? Such a theology would be different from recent attempts to describe a co-suffering God. "Misery loves company" is not a sufficient basis for describing the ultimate power of life and hope in the universe. But a God unacquainted with suffering would be like those tediously smiling Christians who inflict their self-righteousness on us with a cheery "Jesus loves me, are you born again, have a good day!"

Perhaps a new theology would begin by refusing to be awed by violence, by refusing to grant it power. This would be possible only when women and men refuse to cooperate in the ways of violence. No mother's blessing would attend her child's going off to war. No father's smile would greet the militaristic politician. No priest's pardon would hide the battering husband's sin. No professor's pride would sanction the cutting, competitive barb. No physician's fear of malpractice suits would neglect the child's bruises. No police policy would condone the rapist and condemn the woman.

Theology follows life; it does not precede it. Thus there is hope in the essays that follow. They reflect on possibilities already lived, a revolution already begun, even if only here and there amid pervasive violence. But such yeast has power beyond the imagination of those who stand before violence in religious awe.

Introduction

JOANNE CARLSON BROWN / CAROLE R. BOHN

Whenever feminist scholars concerned with religious and ethical issues gather, a common debate invariably surfaces. The question they address is always some form of, Is it possible to be a feminist and retain some attachment to the Christian tradition?

Some radical women among us answer with a resounding No. The more that feminists attempt to recapture women's history, change liturgical practices and religious imagery, and restructure hierarchical ecclesiologies, the more the tradition itself, they claim, will change until eventually it is no longer Christianity. The Christian tradition, continues this line of thought, is so entrenched in and undergirded by patriarchy that without it, the very religion itself would disappear.

Others take a different view. Some among us continue the struggle firmly rooted in the tradition but engaged in radical challenges, challenges going to the root of the tradition. We feel the need to examine the tradition in light of the critiques raised by those who have left and in light of our own dis-ease as we continue to participate in the tradition. What we find is troubling and shaking, and we walk a precariously thin line. In our struggle to remain true to our tradition and to ourselves we are criticized by both sides. Those within the tradition, resistant to any challenge, accuse us of being heretics and say we can no longer claim to be Christian. And those who have left the tradition behind say that we are still trapped by participating in our own oppression since saving a religion based on patriarchy is impossible. Yet we continue to struggle and the debate goes on. The essays that make up this book spring from this ongoing struggle. Our intention in addressing the specific and timely issue of violence against women and children is to focus our attention on the role of Christian theology in undergirding an abusive culture. The theological views confronted here exemplify the way in which the patriarchal roots of the tradition support and perpetuate domestic violence as an acceptable norm.

The volume generally falls into three major sections. We begin by raising theological questions and setting some historical perspective in which to view the issue. Joanne Brown and Rebecca Parker initiate the study with an analysis of the theology of the atonement and the ways in which it makes violence seem appropriate, concluding that glorification of any suffering is glorification of all suffering. Rosemary Radford Ruether, beginning with the early church and moving through the Reformation to witch hunts and contemporary concerns surrounding reproduction, reviews a history of beliefs about women's inferiority and men's dominance in the home. Rita Brock examines Christology, the effects of the father-son imagery, which are so prevalent in the Christian concept of the self, and proposes construction of a new God-child image as a healthier model.

The focus then shifts to more specifically ethical and theological considerations, beginning with Karen Bloomquist's exposition of the many direct as well as subtle ways in which the imbalance of power inherent in patriarchy allows men to act out their power violently. Sheila Redmond looks at the psychological and theological effects of sexual violence on children who live in a "Christian" environment and challenges the ethics of such a Christianity. Mary Hunt introduces the notion of "theological pornography" and thereby goes to the very roots of a Christian theological ethics.

The third section of the book begins with a more psychological perspective, reflecting concern with the effects of violence on the person and its implications for pastoral care. Carole Bohn's view of a "theology of ownership" exposes a basic attitude of those persons in the Christian tradition that not only allows but even encourages violence and deeply damages self-esteem. Demaris Wehr and Polly Young-Eisendrath challenge the psychological notion that separateness is healthy and show how it makes violence against women and children seem reasonable. And Marie Fortune looks at the problems inherent in the Christian notion of suffering as good in itself, suggesting instead that suffering can be transforming toward ending violence.

Beverly Harrison and Carter Heyward's contribution concludes these reflections because they not only offer a challenge to traditional Christian concepts, they integrate their challenge with contemporary feminist thinking.

The concerns and questions raised here are painful to address because they strike at the very heart of our tradition. However, we discuss them because we are convinced that confronting these issues is essential to our religious commitment, our sense of connectedness with the tradition, and to ourselves as feminists. The contributors to this volume represent the women who are asking hard questions, finding painful and difficult answers, and yet are still struggling to remain in that tradition. Some basic reality of life that we find expressed in Christianity keeps us in this struggle.

Whether or not we can continue within the Christian context remains to be seen, and depends largely on how well we can call our sisters and brothers to an honest confrontation with the perversity undergirding the tradition. The questions remain. Is patriarchy inherent in Christian theology? Can we call our "corrected" Christianity Christianity? Is there an essential message of liberation in Christianity that runs counter to patriarchal oppression? Why do we struggle so hard to remain within the tradition? Is there anything worth saving in the Christian tradition? These are essential questions. Yet we cannot begin to answer them until we complete the exorcism of this powerful evil that makes Christianity and violent abuse of women and children synonymous. Patriarchy is the connecting link between the two, and it is the demon challenged in the following pages.

1

For God So Loved the World?

JOANNE CARLSON BROWN / REBECCA PARKER

Women are acculturated to accept abuse. We come to believe that it is our place to suffer. Breaking silence about the victimization of women and the ways in which we have become anesthetized to our violation is a central theme in women's literature, theology, art, social action, and politics. With every new revelation we confront again the deep and painful secret that sustains us in oppression: We have been convinced that our suffering is justified.

THEOLOGY AND ABUSE:
WOMEN'S EXPERIENCE

Our acculturation to abuse is manifested in our blindness to the near-constant repression of our power, our rights, and our lives that occurs in most cultures. In North America many women agree with the men who say that women are not oppressed. They do not see the brutal murders of thirty-six young women in Seattle as a sign of the culture nor understand that the federal government's cutting $7 billion from food stamp programs is evidence that women are not valued since 85 percent of the recipients of food stamps in the United States are women and children. In many parts of the world, cultural tradition dictates that women are second-class citizens: men eat first, are educated first, and make decisions for women. Kumari Jayawardene, a Sri Lankan political scientist and feminist, has commented, "Actually, you know, women really don't understand that they are exploited. When I talk with women's groups I realize this. One day an old woman spoke up and said that she agreed with everything I had said about the situation of women, but that women 'must still have fear and shame, for such are their qualities.' "[1] While we may recognize and reject situations in which there are layers of oppression—as there are for ethnic minority women in North America and poor women in Third World countries—we may still find ourselves so accepting of our own place as helpmate that we cannot see that we are denied our full humanity because we are women. Our acculturation to abuse leads us to keep silent for years about experiences of sexual abuse, to not report rape, to stay in marriages in which we are battered, to give up creative efforts, to expend all our energy in the support of other lives and never in support of our own, to accept it when a man interrupts us, to punish ourselves if we are successful, to deny so habitually our right to self-determination that we do not feel we have an identity unless it is given to us by someone else.

Christianity has been a primary—in many women's lives *the* primary—force in shaping our acceptance of abuse. The central image of Christ on the cross as the savior of the world communicates the message that suffering is redemptive. If the best person who ever lived gave his life for others, then, to be of value we should likewise sacrifice ourselves. Any sense that we have a right to care for our own needs is in conflict with being a faithful follower of Jesus. Our suffering for others will save the world. The message is complicated further by the theology that says Christ suffered in obedience to his Father's will. Divine child abuse is paraded as salvific and the child who suffers "without even raising a voice" is lauded as the hope of the world. Those whose lives have been deeply shaped by the Christian tradition feel that self-sacrifice and obedience are not only virtues but the definition of a faithful identity. The promise of resurrection persuades us to endure pain, humiliation, and violation of our sacred rights to self-determination, wholeness, and freedom. Throughout the Scriptures is the idea that Jesus died for our sins. Did he? Is there not another way for sins to be forgiven? Why an idea of original sin? Christianity has functioned to perpetuate the Fall, for without it there is no need for a savior. Mary Daly argues that imitation of this savior is exactly what is desired:

> The qualities that Christianity idealizes, especially for women, are also those of a victim: sacrificial love, passive acceptance of suffering, humility, meekness, etc. Since these are the qualities idealized in Jesus "who died

2

for our sins," his functioning as a model reinforces the scapegoat syndrome for women.[2]

That victimization is precisely what is perpetuated by this theology can be seen particularly in women's experiences in both the church and society, where women have been assigned the suffering-servant role. Our full personhood as well as our rights have been denied us. We have been labeled the sinful ones, the other; and even when we are let in, so to speak, we are constantly reminded of our inferior status through language, theological concepts of original sin, and perpetual virginity—all of which relate to sex, for which, of course, women are responsible.

In order for us to become whole we must reject the culture that shapes our abuse and disassociate ourselves from the institutions that glorify our suffering. This leads to the conclusion that in order to be liberated we must leave the church, make our exodus from the halls of the oppressor.

Many women, however, even when conscious of the church's contribution to our suffering, do not leave. We stay in the institution. Feminist theologians who attempt to rework the tradition by finding feminist undercurrents and countercultures, doing new quests for the historical feminist Jesus, and writing women back into the Bible and the tradition (the *Inclusive Language Lectionary* is a good example) are trying valiantly to "fix" the institution so that they can remain in it. They enter the ordained ministry in order to "redeem" the church, but they pay so high a personal, emotional, and psychological price that they begin to resemble the very people they want to redeem. All the while, they call to their crucified lord to understand their suffering and support them in their times of trial and martyrdom.

The women who stay are as surely victimized and abused as any battered woman. The reasons given by women who stay in the church are the same as those coming from women who remain in battering situations: they don't mean it; they said they were sorry and would be better; they need me/us; we can fix it if we just try harder and are better; I'd leave but how can I survive outside; we have nowhere else to go. Despite all the correctives taught by liberation theology on how to interpret suffering, this Christian theology with atonement at the center still encourages martyrdom and victimization. It pervades our society. Our internalization of this theology traps us in an almost unbreakable cycle of abuse. Our continuing presence in the church is a sign of the depth of our oppression.

3

The only legitimate reason for women to remain in the church will be if the church were to condemn as anathema the glorification of suffering. Only if the church is the place where cycles of abuse are named, condemned, and broken can it be a haven of blessing and a place of peace for women. That the church is such a place is not clearly evident. Whether Christianity in essence frees or imprisons is the issue that must be considered.

This essay will explore the question, Can the case be made that it is contrary to the gospel to maintain that suffering is redemptive? Our approach is theological, not biblical, and focuses on the issue of the atonement. Classical views of the atonement have, in diverse ways, asserted that Jesus' suffering and death is fundamental to our salvation. Critical traditions have formulated the issue of redemption in different terms but still have not challenged the central problem of the atonement—Jesus' suffering and death, and God's responsibility for that suffering and death. Why we suffer is not a fundamentally different question from why Jesus suffered. It may be that this fundamental tenet of Christianity—Christ's suffering and dying *for us*—upholds actions and attitudes that accept, glorify, and even encourage suffering. Perhaps until we challenge and reject this idea we will never be liberated. And if this glorification of suffering is so central to Christianity itself, perhaps our redemption and liberation, particularly as oppressed people, will be obtained only by leaving.

THE CLASSICAL TRADITION

Jesus died on the cross to save us from sin. This is what the penal theory of the atonement affirms. In classical orthodox theology, the death of Jesus is required by God to make God's plan of salvation effective. Doctrinal standards assert that there was no way more effective, perhaps even no alternative to Jesus' death. Without the death of Jesus we would not be saved. Though there are many different interpretations of *how* we are saved by the death of Jesus, there is no classical theory of the atonement that questions the necessity of Jesus' suffering. And, though the way in which suffering gives birth to redemption is diversely understood, every theory of the atonement commends suffering to the disciple. The Christian is to "be like Jesus"—and imitation of Christ is first and foremost obedient willingness to endure pain.

Three strands of tradition are usually identified as being at the core

4

of the classical views of the atonement. The "Christus Victor" tradition sees the death of Jesus as a mortal confrontation with the powers of evil that oppress human life. Jesus' death represents the apparent triumph of evil, but his resurrection from the dead reveals that God is the greater power whose purpose will finally prevail. Redemption is liberation from evil forces that is brought about by the force of God. The "satisfaction" theory of the atonement says that Jesus died to "pay the price" or "bear the punishment" for human sin. He dies in our place to satisfy God's sense of justice. By his death, a satisfactory payment or sacrifice is offered to God and the barrier of God's wrath is removed. Redemption is accomplished when God is freed from the requirements of "his" honor and is able to relate to human beings with mercy without, so to speak, compromising "his" principles that the sinner should suffer. The "moral influence" theory of the atonement places the barrier to our redemption not in God's nature but in human nature. People's hearts are hardened against mercy; they are unable to see or accept it. Jesus' death on the cross is a divine demonstration of the magnitude of God's mercy. God loves us so much "he" is even willing to die for us. We are to behold the cross and be moved to faith and trust in God, persuaded to accept mercy and dedicate ourselves to obedience to God's will. Each of these theories of the atonement needs to be examined for what it says about suffering, what it counsels the believer to do with regard to his or her own exposures to suffering, and what it says about the nature of God.

The Christus Victor Tradition

The Christus Victor theory of the atonement says that suffering is a prelude to triumph and is in itself an illusion. In some early forms of this view of the atonement, Jesus is imagined as bait for Satan, who seeks to devour human beings. When death swallows up Jesus he gains entrance into the underworld. Confronted with God in hell, Satan is overwhelmed, and the divine light casts darkness from its throne. Gregory of Nyssa, for example, explains,

> Since the hostile power was not going to enter into relations with a God present unveiled or endure his appearance in heavenly glory therefore God . . . concealed himself under the veil of our nature, in order that, as happens with greedy fishes, together with the bait of the flesh the hook of the Godhead might also be swallowed and so through life passing over

into death and the light arising in the darkness that which is opposed to life and light might be brought to nought.[3]

As a mythic drama this atonement story is a tale of hope, with antecedents in Greek stories about Persephone's escape from the evil lord of the underworld bringing Spring with her, and of Orpheus's journey to the underworld to rescue Eurydice. But its charm ends here. By incorporating the actual death of Jesus into a mythic framework, his suffering and death are retold as divine trickery, part of a larger plot to deceive the deceiver. The death of Jesus is merely a ploy, a sleight of hand, an illusion.

More sophisticated theologies that have their roots in this dramatic framework spiritualize the struggle. The journey to the underworld becomes the believer's journey into the dark night of the soul, where God is eclipsed. But this soul journey is part of what is necessary for salvation: all the evil, unfaith, and barrenness in the self must be encountered with the trust that the light of God's presence will finally triumph. Jesus' death becomes a paradigm for a stage in a psychological process that is to be patiently endured. Matthew Fox, discussing the spiritual journey through darkness, writes, "Salvation, we learn from the Via Negativa, is not a salvation *from pain* but *through pain.*"[4] He continues,

All sinking usually has a note of panic about it, and the Via Negativa, which calls us to the deepest sinkings of all, is no exception. Here the refusal to trust, to trust the buoyancy of the water, of the darkness, of the pain, of the nothingness . . . all this is sinful because it stifles our spiritual growth.[5]

When whatever psychological value exists in facing one's inner darkness on the path to greater wholeness and healing is equated with the real death of Jesus, the meaning of suffering is obscured. Fox gives Jesus' actual death as an example to inspire spiritual "letting go" and goes on to blur the distinction between psychological struggle and the sufferings of the poor "who must face their darkness more directly than the comfortable."[6] In a theological effort to show evil and darkness as not ultimately true, the death of Jesus becomes not ultimately real.

The believer whose thoughts and feelings have been shaped by a tradition that teaches or ritualizes in liturgy the Christus Victor view may interpret her or his suffering in this light. In response to suffering it will be said, Be patient, something good will come of this. The believer is persuaded to endure suffering as a prelude to new life. God is pictured as working through suffering, pain, and even death to fulfill "his" divine purpose. When suffering comes it may be looked upon as a gift, and the believer will ask, Where is God leading me? What does God have in store for me? In this tradition, God is the all-powerful determiner of every event in life, and every event is part of a bigger picture—a plan that will end with triumph. When people say things such as, God had a purpose in the death of the six million Jews, the travesty of this theology is revealed.

Such a theology has devastating effects on human life. The reality is that victimization never leads to triumph. It can lead to extended pain if it is not refused or fought. It can lead to destruction of the human spirit through the death of a person's sense of power, worth, dignity, or creativity. It can lead to actual death. By denying the reality of suffering and death, the Christus Victor theory of the atonement defames all those who suffer and trivializes tragedy.

The Satisfaction Tradition

The satisfaction theory of the atonement as formulated by Anselm says that "the Father desired the death of the Son, because he was not willing that the world should be saved in any other way."[7] Because of sin, humanity owed a debt to God which it could not pay. Only by the death of God's own Son could God receive satisfaction. In Anselm's view, God's desire for justice and God's desire to love are in conflict. While there is value in Anselm's claim that love and justice cannot be separated, his view of justice is not that wrong should be righted but that wrongs should be punished.

> Let us . . . consider whether it were proper for God to put away sins by compassion alone, without any payment of the honor taken from him. To remit sin in this manner is nothing else than not to punish: and since it is not right to cancel sin without compensation or punishment: if it be not punished, then it is passed by undischarged. It is not fitting for God to pass over anything in his kingdom undischarged. It is therefore not proper for God thus to pass over sin unpunished.[8] . . . So then, everyone who sins ought to pay back the honor of which he has robbed God and this is the satisfaction which every sinner owes to God.[9]

God's demand that sin be punished is fulfilled by the suffering of the innocent Jesus, whose holiness is crowned by his willingness to be perfectly obedient to his father's will. God is portrayed as the one who cannot reconcile "himself" to the world because "he" has been royally offended by sin, so offended that no human being can do anything to overcome "his" sense of offense. Like Lear, God remains estranged from the children God loves because God's honor must be preserved. God's position is tragic, and it is to free God that the Son submits to death, sacrificing himself, it is imagined, out of overwhelming love for the two alienated parties: God and the human family.

The idea that justice is established through adequate punishment has been questioned by theologians from Anselm's time to the present, though the satisfaction theory has remained the dominant theory of the atonement. The primary criticism is that this theory presents God as a tyrant. Walter Rauschenbusch comments, "The worst form of leaving the naked unclothed, the hungry unfed, and the prisoners uncomforted, is to leave people under a despotic conception of God and the universe; and what will the Son of Man do to us theologians when we gather at the day of doom?"[10] As Rauschenbusch asserts, "Our universe is not a despotic monarchy with God above the starry canopy and ourselves down here; it is a spiritual commonwealth with God in the midst of us."[11]

Anselm uses medieval forensic categories in his construction of a theology that reflects the existing social order—one that operated through coercion and terror. As Rauschenbusch rightly critiqued, "A conception of God which describes him as sanctioning the present order and utilizing it in order to sanctify its victims through their suffering, without striving for its overthrow, is repugnant to our moral sense."[12] But it is precisely this sanctioning of suffering which is the legacy of the satisfaction theory of atonement.

Suffering is sanctioned as an experience that frees others, perhaps even God. The imitator of Christ, which every faithful person is exhorted to be, can find herself choosing to endure suffering because she has become convinced that through her pain another whom she loves will escape pain. The disciple's role is to suffer in the place of others, as Jesus suffered for us all. But this glorification of suffering as salvific, held before us daily in the image of Jesus hanging from the cross, encourages women who are being abused to be more concerned about their victimizer than about themselves. Children who are abused are forced most keenly to face the conflict between the claims of a parent who professes love and the inner self which protests violation.

8

When a theology identifies love with suffering, what resources will its culture offer to such a child? And when parents have an image of a God righteously demanding the total obedience of "his" son—even obedience to death—what will prevent the parent from engaging in divinely sanctioned child abuse? The image of God the father demanding and carrying out the suffering and death of his own son has sustained a culture of abuse and led to the abandonment of victims of abuse and oppression. Until this image is shattered it will be almost impossible to create a just society.

Yet another dimension of the satisfaction theory of the atonement needs to be addressed. Though Anselm's formulation of the satisfaction theory is influenced by medieval legal concepts, the theory has deep roots in biblical images of sacrifice. In the liturgy, hymnody, and practical piety of the church, these images are continually evoked. While the biblical view of the power of blood sacrifice is complex, four major themes may be identified:[13]

1. Blood protects. Blood circumcision and the blood of the passover lamb are seen as having power to ward off the destroyer (see Exod. 4:24–26; 12:27).

2. Blood intercedes. In the Book of Genesis, Abel's blood is said to "cry out to God" (Gen. 4:10); and this idea that spilled blood has a power greater than language to attract God's attention is taken up in Heb. 12:24: "But you have come . . . to Jesus, the mediator of a new covenant, and to the sprinkled blood that speaks more graciously than the blood of Abel" (see also Isa. 56:7, in which sacrifice is associated with prayer).

3. Blood establishes covenant. The covenant with Abraham (Genesis 15), the Covenant at Sinai (Exod. 24:3–11), and the "new Covenant" (Matt. 26:28; 1 Cor. 10:16, 11:25; Heb. 9:16–18) are all sealed or established with the letting of blood. Further, membership in the house of Israel is established for men by the letting of blood that occurs in the circumcision ritual.

4. Blood makes atonement. The ritual sacrifice of whole and unblemished animals at the altar serves to make peace between God and the sinful community. The prophets emphasized that true or effective sacrifice has to do with the right attitude on the part of the one who offers. Sacrifice as magic was rejected, and "spiritual" sacrifice began to replace ritual sacrifice. Through the prophetic critique of false sacrifice it became clear to the religious .

imagination of Israel that righteousness was the only true sacrifice. But who is righteous enough to offer completely effective sacrifice? The significance of Jesus as the one true sacrifice must be understood in this light. Jesus' death was, in the biblical tradition, God's gracious offering of the perfect sacrifice, which none of us was capable of presenting.

Through all these varied images of the "power of let blood," the question must be asked, Why does blood have the power to protect life, establish relationship, restore life, speak with silent eloquence? The answer to such a question lies in the history of ritual practices and in the grounding of symbolic elements in life experience. The holy power of blood comes from the understanding of blood as essential to life. Its power is the power of life. Beyond this, however, the power of *let* blood—flowing, released, spilled blood—has an additional source in human experience. The slaughter of animals means food that will nurture human life; this is one form in which let blood is a sign that life will be sustained. But there is another form of flowing blood that encompasses all the imagistic power of blood in the Old Testament; blood that is a sign of sustenance, intimate/communal relationship, and new life. That form is woman's blood, both menstrual blood and birth blood.

Ironically, in the biblical tradition menstrual blood is a sign of ritual uncleanness. Here, the student of religious symbolism must pause. Studies have revealed that various forms of ritual bloodletting are imitations, by members of a male cult, of women's bodily experience. Circumcision, for example, occurs in many cultures, not only the ancient Hebrew, and is often spoken of as "men's menstruation."[14] This would indicate that the notion of "flowing blood" has its roots in cultural efforts by men to take unto themselves power that belongs to women. The imitation by men of women's bodily power has almost universally been accompanied by the subjugation of women.[15] Ritual exclusion of menstruating women and women who have given birth is a sign that sacred imagery has been stolen. This analysis suggests that the religious imagery of the atonement is founded upon the robbery and subsequent defamation/degradation of women's experience.[16] The religious imagery of Jesus' blood carries an implied, silent devaluation of women. Jesus becomes the true mother who gives us new birth through his body and feeds us with his flesh. In medieval mysticism, this symbolism becomes blatant. Jesus is imaged as a mother: "His outspread arms will invite you to embrace him, his naked breasts will feed you with the milk of sweetness to console you."[17] And his wounded body becomes a womb to which the believer can crawl back:

> Those unsearchable riches of your glory, Lord, were hidden in your secret place in heaven until the soldier's spear opened the side of your Son, our Lord and Savior on the cross, and from it flowed the mysteries of our redemption. Now we may not only thrust our fingers or our hand into his side, like Thomas, but through that open door may enter whole, O Jesus, even into your heart.[18]

While many may argue that the primitive origins of blood sacrifice are not relevant, they do continue to hold power over us. Their subtle influence is pervasive in women's experience. Having an understanding of Jesus as our new mother, who gives life through death, serves to devalue our natural mothers, who give life through life, and communicates to every woman that she is inferior to man. Can an image offer redemption while perpetuating devaluation? Or can it speak of justice when its symbolic origins involved subjugation? The symbol itself is a form of abuse.

The Moral Influence Tradition

The moral influence theory of the atonement began with Abelard questioning the satisfaction theory:

> If [the] sin of Adam was so great that it could be expiated only by the death of Christ, what expiation will avail for the act of murder committed against Christ, and for the many great crimes committed against him or his followers? How did the death of his innocent Son so please God the Father that through it he should be reconciled to us?[19]

In answering this question Abelard rejected the satisfaction theory of the atonement in favor of saying that the barrier preventing reconciliation between God and human beings is not in God but in human beings. The problem is that we need to be persuaded faithfully to believe in God's overwhelming mercy. The evidence that should persuade us is that Jesus was willing to die for us. He has shown that he holds our souls in such high esteem that we should recognize our forgiven and loved condition and in gratitude commit ourselves to obedience like his.

The moral influence theory is founded on the belief that an innocent, suffering victim and only an innocent, suffering victim for whose suffering we are in some way responsible has the power to confront us with our guilt and move us to a new decision. This belief has subtle and terrifying connections as to how victims of violence can be viewed. Theoretically, the victimization of Jesus should suffice for our moral edification, but, in fact, in human history, races, classes, and women have been victimized while at the same time their victimization has been heralded as a persuasive reason for inherently sinful men to become more righteous. The suffering of ethnic minorities and the poor has been graphically described, along with the suffering of Jesus, in sermonic efforts to move the powerful to repentance and responsibility. Sometimes this amounts to using the victims for someone else's edification. But, most perniciously, it is the victimization of women that is tied to a psychology of redemption.

Christian ethicist Helmut Thielicke provides a particularly clear example of how theories of atonement find expression in sexual politics. His view is that woman's sexuality is by nature holistic and vulnerable. He images women as holy and sees women as intrinsically good in their sexual nature, in which sexual desire is completely integrated with the heart and with a desire for faithfulness. He also sees woman as intrinsically vulnerable because her integrated sexual nature is such that if she is sexually intimate with a man she becomes bonded for life with that man. He sees men, on the other hand, as intrinsically destructive in their sexuality—originally sinful, you might say. Men's sexual energy is energy to violate and destroy. It is unfaithful, also, because the man's sexual feeling is an alienated, unintegrated part of himself, making him tend toward polygamy. In Thielicke's view, men are saved from their inherent destructiveness when they are moved by the suffering of victimized women. When a man sees the holiness and fragility of woman, he may be persuaded to repent of his destructive behavior, discipline himself to be obedient to love's demand, and thereby become a saved, holy, good human being himself.[20]

In this twentieth-century formulation of Christian ethics, woman is cast as a Christ figure; she is imagined to be a victim who does not deserve the suffering that comes to her. Thielicke writes of a woman, "She can exist and be herself only as long as the other person who has become the one and only for her preserves the bond in which she has invested her being."[21] Man's faithfulness is required or she will cease to exist. In this pattern of relationship, communion is maintained through the threat of death. The actual deaths or violations of women are part of the system just as necessarily as the death of Jesus is part of the system that asks for us to be "morally persuaded" to be faithful to God. The burden is on the believer to redeem Jesus' death from tragedy, but the believer cannot be redeemed without the example of the tragedy. This is the kind of double bind in which women find themselves in Christian culture. We must be viewed as vulnerable to victimization and loved not because of who we are but to save another from the guilt of being himself with us. If a man is himself, he destroys us. If he saves us, he must contradict his own nature. The hostility that pervades such a view of women is intense and hidden. But it is similar to the hostility that this form of Christian theology creates in the relationship between human beings and God. We can protect God from our violent rejection by disciplining ourselves, but it is the vulnerable holy One who is to blame for our having to construct rigid systems of self-control. God must be hated—just as women are hated. The moral influence theories of the atonement sanctify love/hate relationships. Redemption is not to be found in intimate relationships; only vicious cycles of violence may be found. Holding over people's heads the threat that if they do not behave someone will die requires occasional fulfillment of the threat. The threat of death, however, should not be called moral persuasion but should be identified as the most pernicious and evil form of coercion and terror.

How can we explain the condition of women, and others who are the chosen victims in a society, who live in constant fear of rape, murder, attack, verbal assault, insult, and the denial of rights and opportunities except as a condition of terrorization? To glorify victims of terrorization by attributing to them a vulnerability that warrants protection by the stronger is to cloak the violation. Those who seek to protect are guilty. Justice occurs when terrorization stops, not when the condition of the terrorized is lauded as a preventive influence.

THE CRITICAL TRADITION

Many theologians of the modern and post-modern period have directed severe criticism at the traditional atonement concepts. Biblical concepts of suffering as traditionally interpreted have been reexamined and found not only wanting but also contributing to oppression. These critical theologians have claimed that classical atonement theories have been used to maintain the status quo and exonerate the purposes of a tyrannical God. They have seen that their task is to free God from the charge of Divine Oppressor and then join with this liberated God in laying the ax to the root of oppression, that is, to end the suffering that is at the heart of oppression. This has been done by insisting that all suffering must be regarded as negative and not ordained by God. All, that is, except Jesus'! This is where the critical traditions fall short of pushing the challenge to its logical conclusion.

Three trends in the twentieth-century critique of classical atonement theories may be identified. One trend criticizes the traditional view of God as impassive and asserts that God suffers with us. A second interprets suffering as an essential and inevitable part of the historical process of the struggle for liberation. A third trend radically critiques the notion of redemptive suffering but insists on retaining the cross as an image of liberation.

The Suffering God

Ronald Goetz has suggested that the notion of the "Suffering God" is becoming a new orthodoxy in the twentieth century.[22] He says that until this century the orthodox position affirmed again and again the doctrine of God as immovable and impassible, but twentieth-century theologians from even radically diverse schools of thought have forwarded the image and concept of God as one who suffers passionately what the world suffers. Goetz lists those he would characterize as modern theopaschite thinkers: "Barth, Berdyaev, Bonhoeffer, Brunner, Cobb, Cone and liberation theologians generally, Kung, Moltmann, Reinhold Niebuhr, Pannenberg, Ruether and feminist theologians generally, Temple, Teilhard and Unamuno."[23] We would add to this list Edgar Sheffield Brightman and the personalists, and process theologians in general.

In our view the emergence of the notion that God suffers with us is theological progress. God as one who experiences, feels, and knows life, as one intimately bound up with the creation in all its tragedy and turmoil, resurrects God from the grave of stony impassibility. To live is to experience, and, finally, the doctrine of an impassible God cannot be reconciled to the doctrine of a *living* God. To see God as the "fellow sufferer who understands" is to draw God close to all those who suffer and give divine companionship to the friendless.

We would not reject the image of God as a Suffering God and would

14

welcome the demise of that distant, impassive patriarch in the clouds who is beyond being affected by the turmoil below. The advent of the Suffering God changes the entire face of theology, but it does not necessarily offer liberation for those who suffer. A closer examination of one form of Suffering God theology will reveal that this apparently new image of God still produces the same answers to the question, How shall I interpret and respond to the suffering that occurs in my life? And the answer again is, Patiently endure; suffering will lead to greater life.

Edgar Sheffield Brightman, a Boston personalist[24] of the 1920s and 1930s, proposed one of the clearest doctrines of a Suffering God. His definition of God is captured in this passage:

> God is a conscious Person of perfect good will. He is the source of all value and so is worthy of worship and devotion. He is the creator of all other persons and gives them the power of free choice. . . . There is within him, in addition to his reason and his active creative will, a passive element which enters into every one of his conscious states, as sensation, instinct, and impulse enter into ours, and constitutes a problem for him. This element we call The Given. The evils of life and the delays in the attainment of value, insofar as they come from God and not from human freedom, are thus due to his nature, yet not wholly to his deliberate choice. His will and reason acting on The Given produce the world and achieve value in it.[25]

This definition may be put more concisely in the following terms:

> God is a Person supremely conscious, supremely valuable, and supremely creative, yet limited both by the free choices of other persons and by restrictions within his own nature.[26]

In Brightman's view God has limited power, and this limitation is not the result of divine free choice but is imposed by God's very nature. It is the tension within God's self as God responds to the "Given" within Godself. Gradually God is working out God's purpose, as God responds to the Given in a way that will transform/transcend all evil. The reason there is evil is because things just do not fit together. Evil is inherent in the nature of things, what Brightman calls the "cosmic drag." God is unfinished. Suffering occurs because of the conflict between what is and what could be within God. Hence, God participates in the suffering of all the creation, groaning together with the creation in the travail of perfection coming to birth. Brightman says of God,

> He is supreme goodness conquering all obstacles, although slowly and with round about and painful methods. He is a God who suffers and who redeems. He is a finite God, working under the conditions given by his own eternal nature. He is not free to emancipate himself wholly from these conditions, although he is able to accomplish his purpose of achieving good in every situation and is never finally baffled by any problems. He is not responsible for causing the evils of life; he is responsible for dealing with them.[27]

Brightman's identification of the origin of suffering in the conflict between what is and what could be views all suffering as a byproduct of God's progressive creativity. It must be criticized as inadequate for explaining those forms of suffering that are the consequence of blatant injustices committed by human beings, such as slavery, abject poverty, or violence against women.

Brightman's answer to oppressed peoples struggling to interpret their suffering is: God suffers with you, knows, and understands your pain. God suffers actively, not passively, a suffering that knows a change is needed. So must we all become active sufferers.

> One [who is] moved by pity and love, uses every ounce of strength he possesses in fighting disease and disaster, pain and woe of every kind; but he has the insight to see that lamentations over the imperfection of the result would only add to the sufferings of life and consequently he is patient even when his efforts are most unsuccessful. Patient submission to the inevitable is a virtue only when one has gained the right, by one's attitude, to call it inevitable. To ascribe war, crimes, and lawlessness to fate is a cheap and irresponsible patience.[28]

Brightman challenges patient acquiescence before suffering and provides a way to continue to work against oppression when success is not immediate. The atonement is to be understood as support for this struggle. It is in the struggle of Christ on the cross that we see and know that God struggles and suffers for the world's salvation.[29]

Brightman, with critical theologians in general, uses God's suffering with us to call human beings to suffer with one another for liberation, suggesting that "suffering with" is itself a redeeming action. The identification in Suffering God theology of solidarity with redemption should be questioned. Bearing the burden with another does not take

16

the burden away. Sympathetic companionship makes suffering more bearable, but the friendship between slaves, for example, does not stop the master from wielding the lash. Goetz also makes this observation:

> There is a certain immediate psychological comfort in the notion that God does not require of us a suffering that he himself will not endure. However, if this comfort is to be any more than a psychological prop, it must show how God's suffering mitigates evil. This explanation has been, to date, curiously lacking in the theodicy of divine self-limitation.[30]

The challenge of how to claim that a suffering God offers not only comfort and companionship but also redemption is perhaps met by the argument that the cross makes relationship where relationship has been lost. It breaks down the dividing wall between suffering humanity and an impassive God and calls disciples to cross the barrier that separates oppressor from oppressed, rich from poor, healthy from sick, into a new humanity in which each takes on the burdens and joys of all in a fellowship of mutual openness and support. Such a passage into community involves being open to one's own pain and the pain of others. Thus it involves being willing to face reality, to feel, to see, instead of to repress feeling and hide from the truth or insulate oneself and ignore the realities of injustice. Such commitment to *live* establishes new community, and it is the establishment of community in which the alienation caused by rejection of suffering is overcome through mutuality that creates justice. The vision of such a community commends itself to all people. The creation of such a community surely does involve individuals choosing to see their intimate connection with those they may have rejected or ignored and choosing to admit those others into the circle of their concern and commitment. Indeed, such commitment involves facing the fact that an image of the self as impassible and immutable to pain blocks a person from being in relationship to others. A God who cannot feel cannot be alive and intimately related to other lives. So also a human being who idealizes the transcendence of emotion and seeks freedom from "being effected" by others cannot be fully alive or intimately related to others. Life is changed by the decision to feel, to be involved, to care, and to not turn away out of offense at or fear of another's suffering. The new community that is brought into being by God's intimate connection to us and by our openness to the life in ourselves and in others claims our attention and indeed has a right to be called redemption.

But a question arises: Even if the creation of communities of just relationship mitigates the evils of oppression, abuse, injustice, and alienation, that is, even if the establishment of *right relationship* is the meaning of *redemption*, how is it that the torturous death of Jesus can be spoken of as initiating this new community? Do we need the death of God incarnate to show us that God is with us in our suffering? Was Jesus' suffering and death required for revelation to occur? Was God not with us in our suffering before the death of Jesus? Did the death really initiate something that did not exist before?

It is true that fullness of life cannot be experienced without openness to all truth, all reality; fullness of life involves feeling the pain of the world. But it is not true that being open to all of life is the equivalent of choosing to suffer. Nor is it right to see the death of Jesus as a symbol for the life-giving power of receptivity to reality.

It is not acceptance of suffering that gives life; it is commitment to life that gives life. The question, moreover, is not, Am I willing to suffer? but Do I desire fully to live? This distinction is subtle and, to some, specious, but in the end it makes a great difference in how people interpret and respond to suffering. If you believe that acceptance of suffering gives life, then your resources for confronting perpetrators of violence and abuse will be numbed.

Jurgen Moltmann, for example, fails to make this distinction and hence continues the traditional presentation of Jesus as one who chose to suffer. He writes, "Jesus himself set out for Jerusalem and actively took the expected suffering upon himself."[31] Moltmann explicitly rejects the interpretation of Jesus' death that says Jesus died because of the "deep rooted evil of other people"[32] and speaks instead of Jesus *inciting violence against himself.*

> Jesus did not suffer passively from the world in which he lived, but incited it against himself by his message and the life he lived. . . . By proclaiming the righteousness of God as the right of those who were rejected and without grace to receive grace, he provoked the hostility of the guardians of the law, . . . he incited the devout against him.[33]

Moltmann's view amounts to blaming the victim. Jesus is responsible for his death on the cross, just as a woman who walks alone at night on a deserted street is to blame when she is raped.

Moltmann's intent is to distinguish between what he calls "active suffering" (i.e., chosen suffering) and acquiescence to suffering viewed as fate. But by continuing a theology that cloaks the perpetrator of violence and calls the choice *for life* a choice *to suffer*, he fails to present a theology capable of moving beyond suffering as fate to be endured.

At issue is not what we choose to endure or accept but what we refuse to relinquish. Redemption happens when people refuse to relinquish respect and concern for others, when people refuse to relinquish fullness of feeling, when people refuse to give up seeing, experiencing, and being connected and affected by all of life. God must be seen as the one who most fully refuses to relinquish life. Lust for life—the insistent zest for experiencing and responding—is what has the power to create community and sustain justice. The ongoing resurrection within us of a passion for life and the exuberant energy of this passion testifies to God's spirit alive in our souls.

By confusing "suffering with" with action that does something about evil instead of asserting that testifying for life is what sustains justice, the Suffering God theologies continue in a new form the traditional piety that sanctions suffering as imitation of the holy one. Because God suffers and God is good, we are good if we suffer. If we are not suffering, we are not good. To be like God is to take on the pain of all. In this form of piety, pain becomes attractive—the more we suffer the more we can believe we approach God. By interpreting Jesus' suffering as a sign that chosen suffering is salvific the Suffering God theology baptizes violence done by people resistant to grace and abundant life, and uses Jesus' death to invite people to be open to all of life. This theology is offensive because it suggests that acceptance of pain is tantamount to love and is the foundation of social action.

There is another motivation for our commitment to live in solidarity with others. It is found in the rightness of the claim that burns in every human heart that we are created for life and life abundant. Life calls us to not abandon one another to the grave, and it is the claim of life that should inspire us to remain faithful to one another—not the glorification of pain.

The Necessity of Suffering

The second major trend in twentieth-century critiques of classical atonement theories is that suffering is an essential part of the process of liberation. A version of this is seen in Brightman's theology: God is unfinished, and the creation is slowly moving toward a final harvest of righteousness. More recent theologians have not shared the Social

Darwinism of early twentieth-century optimistic, progressive theology, but in a different form have insisted, nevertheless, that suffering be understood within the larger context of historical processes of change. Returning to biblical themes of hope, they interpret the crucifixion of Jesus as a sign that before the dawn of a new age a period of struggle, violence, sacrifice, and pain will inevitably occur. In liberation and critical theologies the suffering of Jesus becomes a symbol for the conflicts that occur when people fight for new and more just social forms. The old must pass away before the new comes, and in its death throes the old lashes out against the new. The martyrs of the revolution are the sign that the beast is dying. Their blood gives hope, because it reveals the crisis that is at hand. Furthermore, violence against the vanguards of a new age is to be accepted. Acceptance witnesses against the perpetrator of violence and ennobles the victim. Martin Luther King, Jr., for example, accepted the inevitability of the violence directed against the civil rights movement and saw it as the responsibility of people in the movement to bear the suffering in order to transform the situation.

> Suffering can be a most creative and powerful social force. . . . The non-violent say that suffering becomes a powerful social force when you willingly accept that violence on yourself, so that self-suffering stands at the center of the nonviolent movement and the individuals involved are able to suffer in a creative manner, feeling that unearned suffering is redemptive, and that suffering may serve to transform the social situation.[34]

King's view is similar to the "moral influence" theory of the atonement: unjust suffering has the power to move the hearts of perpetrators of violence. The problem with this theology is that it asks people to suffer for the sake of helping evildoers see their evil ways. It puts concern for the evildoer ahead of concern for the victim of evil. It makes victims the servants of the evildoers' salvation.

King sees suffering as necessary because the very suffering of the victims of injustice will cause change by inspiring evildoers to change. Archbishop Oscar Romero reflected similarly:

> The only violence that the Gospel admits is violence to oneself. When Christ lets himself be killed, that is violence—letting himself be killed. Violence to oneself is more effective than violence against others. It is very easy to kill, especially when one has weapons, but how hard it is to let oneself be killed for love of the people![35]

This martyrdom theology ignores the fact that the perpetrators of violence against "the faithful" have a choice and, instead, suggests to the faithful that when someone seeks to silence them with threats or violence, they are in a situation of blessedness. Romero wrote,

> To each of us Christ is saying: if you want your life and mission to be fruitful like mine, do like me. Be converted into a seed that lets itself be buried. Let yourself be killed. Do not be afraid. Those who shun suffering will remain alone. No one is more alone than the selfish. But if you give your life out of love for others, as I give mine for all, you will reap a great harvest. You will have the deepest satisfactions. Do not fear death or threats. The Lord goes with you.[36]

Instead of making the straightforward observation that those in power resist change by using violence to silence and terror to intimidate any who question an unjust status quo, these theologians are saying that suffering is a positive and necessary part of social transformation. The violence of those who resist change becomes mythologized as part of a divinely ordained process of transformation, exemplified through Jesus' death and resurrection. In this mythologizing, historical realities are clouded, as Jon Sobrino rightly observes:

> There has been a tendency to isolate the cross from the historical course that led Jesus to it by virtue of his conflicts with those who held political religious power. In this way the cross has been turned into nothing more than a paradigm of the suffering to which all human beings are subject insofar as they are limited beings. This has given rise to a mystique of suffering rather than to a mystique of following Jesus, whose historical career led to the historical cross.[37]

The Negativity of Suffering

The third trend in twentieth-century critical traditions' view of the atonement is perhaps the most radical. It rejects the concept that human suffering can have positive or redemptive aspects. This trend is represented by such people as Jon Sobrino, William R. Jones, and Carter Heyward. Their critique is radical in the sense of the questions raised regarding theodicy.

> The whole question of God finds its ultimate concretion in the problem of suffering. The question rises out of the history of suffering in the world, but it finds its privileged moment on the cross: if the Son is innocent and yet put to death, then who or what exactly is God?[38]

In his book, *Is God a White Racist?* Jones searches for the answer to the how and why of suffering, particularly ethnic suffering. He recognizes four features of ethnic suffering: maldistribution, negative quality, enormity, and noncatastrophic character. From these he postulates what he terms "divine racism." The question of divine racism arises when this ethnic suffering is joined with a particular interpretation of God's sovereignty over human history. Is God responsible for evil and suffering, and does this responsibility fit in with our traditional concept of a benevolent God? Some feminist theologians have challenged the traditional understanding and interpretation of the suffering servant and the suffering and death of Jesus. Most reject the traditional use of the crucifixion to bless the victimization of women.

> Women are particularly sensitive to the way in which the suffering servant image has functioned in the Christian tradition, for we have invariably played that role within the family and vis-à-vis man in the larger society. . . . And in carrying the sins of the male half of the world on their shoulders, women are discovering that they have allowed men to escape from the responsibility of bearing their own burdens and coming to terms with their own sin and guilt. . . . Thus the suffering servant role model, a product of the patriarchal consciousness, has functioned to perpetuate that very dichotomy and alienation between human beings that the tradition claims to overcome. In accepting that particular interpretation of the Christ event as normative for their lives, women have participated in their own crucifixion. As feminists, we must exorcise that image from our midst in order to discover the roots of that true reconciliation which can only come about between equals.[39]

But even while recognizing the link between Jesus' suffering and theirs, most feminist theologians have been reluctant to criticize the idea of the atonement. Carter Heyward, in her book *The Redemption of God*, comes closest to this type of critique by challenging and rejecting a notion of a sadistic God. But even with all these radical critiques and theodicies, these theologians continue to save the cross as a viable, meaningful, indeed necessary, part of what Christianity is.

Jon Sobrino, in *Christology at the Crossroads*, best represents this idea, especially among Latin American liberation theologians. He radically critiques traditional views of the cross, which have spiritualized the impact and taken away the scandal. He asks what justification there is for a God who allows the sinfulness of the world to kill his son and, by implication, other human beings as well.[40] But Sobrino goes on to point out the positive aspect he sees in the cross:

On the positive side the cross presents a basic affirmation about God. It says that on the cross God himself is crucified. The Father suffers the death of his Son and takes upon himself all the sorrow and pain of history. This ultimate solidarity with humanity reveals God as a God of love in a real and credible way rather than in an idealistic way. From the ultimate depths of history's negative side, this God of love thereby opens up the possibility of hope and a future.[41]

This idea is closely related to the suffering God idea discussed above, but it carries the concept a bit further. The cross and the suffering and death of Jesus are necessary for God to have any solidarity with the poor and oppressed of the world. Without it God cannot be the compassionate, loving God we have posited. Without the cross there is no Christianity.

Latin American liberation theologians have focused on the cross as an example of commitment to justice and liberation. It is the result of working for justice. It is the example of love and hence of life. It enables us to endure. These ideas encompass each of the trends of the critical tradition, and, in a time of severe persecution such as Christians in Latin America are currently experiencing, it is understandable. There is a need to understand a situation of senseless suffering and death and to remain courageously committed to the struggle in the face of the despair and grief such suffering brings. But to sanction the suffering and death of Jesus, even when calling it unjust, so that God can be active in the world only serves to perpetuate the acceptance of the very suffering against which one is struggling. The glorification of anyone's suffering allows the glorification of all suffering. To argue that salvation can only come through the cross is to make God a divine sadist and a divine child abuser.

William R. Jones has a stronger critique of the cross than does Sobrino. His critique begins with the suffering servant motif, which he sees involved in many black justifications of black suffering. Jones states that the suffering servant motif cannot deal with noncatastrophic suffering, such as has faced the black race, because an exaltation-liberation event must occur for the interpretation of deserved punishment to be dismissed. The suffering must cease, the suffering servant must be vindicated, and the suffering must be replaced by liberation.[42] This, says Jones, has clearly not happened in the black situation. He expresses this especially in terms of the crucifixion-resurrection event, which is traditionally viewed by Christians as *the* liberation event.

To speak of the cross, in the Christian tradition, has been to speak of
human redemption, their salvation and deliverance. But the fact of
oppression *after* the occurrence of the normative event of reconciliation
raises special questions.[43]

Hence Jones insists on viewing all suffering as negative, for if we
define an instance of suffering as positive or necessary for salvation, we
are persuaded to endure it. This has been used too long by the
oppressors to both justify their positions and release them from any
responsibility for the oppressed's condition and suffering. Jones states
that a theology of liberation must provide persuasive grounds for
removing the sanctity and hallowed status from those it seeks to
challenge.[44] Any attempt to eliminate or reduce suffering or to challenge one's condition is, by that very act, a direct challenge to the
appropriateness of that suffering and condition.[45] It is to challenge
God, if one believes in God's responsibility for all things in this world.
It is to call God a white racist.

How can we judge God's motive or character at this point? Jones
looks at the approach of the Hebrew Scripture writers to this critical
issue. He finds that their convictions about the nature of God's future
acts were grounded in the character of God's past and present acts.[46]
What conclusions can be drawn about God by looking at past and
present persistent and ruthlessly enforced suffering of the oppressed?
Unrelieved suffering is explicable if (1) there is no God; (2) God exists
but is not active in human affairs; or (3) God exists and is active in
certain sectors of human history but is absent from the struggle for
liberation. The elimination of oppression is not a priority item on God's
agenda, if it is found there at all. God is clearly an oppressor, a white
racist.[47] This view is theologically impossible if one posits a universally
benevolent God. If one assumes God's intrinsic goodness and justice,
one must do one of two things: (1) adopt a theodicy based on God's
benevolence (Jones sees this as question begging and ultimately skirting
the issues or desperately attempting to justify God's position) or (2) opt
for atheism or, as Jones presents his solution, humanocentric theism.
This humanocentric theism stresses the functional ultimacy of humans
by virtue of their creation and eliminates God's responsibility for the
crimes or errors of human history. This ultimacy is in total conformity
with the sovereignty, purpose, and will of God.[48] It is in respect for
human free will, which God created, that God acts as a persuader

24

rather than a coercer. By becoming human in Jesus of Nazareth, God affirmed that God's activity in human history from then on would be carried out in the activity of particular people.

In this view of God, this humanocentric theism, God is not for the oppressed, in terms of their being "unique objects of God's activity in a manner that differs from persuasion."[49] It is essential for Jones's system that human activity be decisive for one's salvation or liberation. History is open-ended, "capable of supporting either oppression or liberation, racism or brotherhood."[50] This, he argues, does not remove hope from theology; it restores responsibility to humanity. He challenges some of the traditional beliefs of blacks as being, in fact, part of their oppression.[51]

Jones's critique comes closest to naming the problem. He labels all suffering as negative, asserts that the crucifixion is not liberating without the resurrection, and suggests that our cherished beliefs may, in fact, be part of our oppression. But he, too, fails to make the connections among all these ideas. Why is the crucifixion necessary? Does God demand this suffering and death as payment for sin or even as a condition for the forgiveness of sin? Is the question not Is God a racist, but rather, Is God a sadist? And is the identification black people, particularly black women, felt with the suffering Jesus part of their oppression? Again, Jones does not intend to denigrate the suffering and oppression of black people. Jesus is clearly seen as a political messiah for blacks. The condition of black people today signifies Christ's crucifixion. His resurrection signifies black hope.[52] The suffering that Jesus experienced is not being questioned. God's demand, the sacralizing of the suffering, is at issue and is not addressed by Jones.

Carter Heyward makes the most radical departure from traditional views of the atonement. She does so because she approaches the question free from some theological trappings. First, she asserts that Jesus is important if he is only and fully human. She also implies that there is no original sin in the classical sense, hence nothing from which humanity needs to be redeemed. For Heyward, Jesus' death was an evil act done by humans. It was unnecessary, violent, unjust, and final.[53] This leads her to condemn the glorification of suffering found in traditional Christian theology.

> Any theology which is promulgated on an assumption that followers of Jesus, Christians, must welcome pain and death as a sign of faith is

25

constructed upon a faulty hermeneutic of what Jesus was doing and of why he died. This theological masochism is completely devoid of passion. This notion of welcoming, or submitting oneself gladly to, injustice flies in the face of Jesus' own refusal to make concession to unjust relation.[54]

Jesus died because he was a radical who challenged the unjust systems under which he lived. Jesus challenged the theological idea of a sadistic God:

> The image of a Jesus who, in the prophetic tradition of Israel, despised the blasphemous notion of a deity who likes sacrifice, especially *human* sacrifice, can assure us that we are not here to give ourselves up willingly to be crucified for anyone's sake, but rather to struggle together against the injustice of all human sacrifice, including our own.[55]

Heyward, by rejecting the notion of a sadistic God, argues very effectively that this notion is blasphemy. But she fails to identify the traditional doctrine of the atonement as the central reason for the oppressiveness of Christianity. Despite her many unorthodox beliefs, Heyward still locates herself firmly in the Christian tradition and struggles to stay there. It is precisely this struggle that prevents her from labeling Christianity as essentially an abusive theology. She struggles to redeem the doctrine of the atonement. Despite her reimaging of a Jesus who "redeems" by showing us that "salvation" consists in being in an intimate, immediate love relationship with God, has she merely reworked the traditions and called them blasphemous when in reality that blasphemous God, the God who demands sacrifice, that patriarchal God, is the one to be found in the text, is, in fact, the God upon which the entire Christian tradition is built?

CONCLUSION

Christianity is an abusive theology that glorifies suffering. Is it any wonder that there is so much abuse in modern society when the predominant image or theology of the culture is of "divine child abuse"—God the Father demanding and carrying out the suffering and death of his own son? If Christianity is to be liberating for the oppressed, it must itself be liberated from this theology. We must do away with the atonement, this idea of a blood sin upon the whole human race which can be washed away only by the blood of the lamb. This bloodthirsty God is the God of the patriarchy who at the moment controls the whole Judeo-Christian tradition. This raises the key question for oppressed people seeking liberation within this tradition: If we throw out the atonement is Christianity left? Can we call our new creation Christianity even with an asterisk?

We do not need to be saved by Jesus' death from some original sin. We need to be liberated from the oppression of racism, classism, and sexism, that is, from patriarchy. If in that liberation process there is suffering it will be because people with power choose to use their power to resist and oppose the human claim to passionate and free life. Those who seek redemption must dare to live their lives with passion in intimate, immediate love relationships with each other, remembering times when we were not slaves.

Our adventure into freedom is empowered by rejecting and denying the abuse that is the foundation of the throne of sacrifice. We choose to call the new land we enter Christianity if

Christianity is at heart and essence justice, radical love, and liberation.

Jesus is one manifestation of Immanuel but not uniquely so, whose life exemplified justice, radical love, and liberation.

Jesus chose to live a life in opposition to unjust, oppressive cultures. Jesus did not choose the cross but chose integrity and faithfulness, refusing to change course because of threat.

Jesus' death was an unjust act, done by humans who chose to reject his way of life and sought to silence him through death. The travesty of the suffering and death of Jesus is not redeemed by the resurrection.

Jesus was not an acceptable sacrifice for the sins of the whole world, because God does not need to be appeased and demands not sacrifice but justice. To know God is to do justice (Jer. 22:13–16). Peace was not made by the cross. "Woe to those who say Peace, Peace when there is no peace" (Jer. 6:14). No one was saved by the death of Jesus.

Suffering is never redemptive, and suffering cannot be redeemed.

The cross is a sign of tragedy. God's grief is revealed there and everywhere and every time life is thwarted by violence. God's grief is as ultimate as God's love. Every tragedy eternally remains and is eternally mourned. Eternally the murdered scream, Betrayal. Eternally God sings kaddish for the world.

To be a Christian means keeping faith with those who have heard and lived God's call for justice, radical love, and liberation; who have challenged unjust systems both political and ecclesiastical; and who in that struggle have refused to be victims and have refused to cower under the threat of violence, suffering, and death. Fullness of life is attained in moments of decision for such faithfulness and integrity. When the threat of death is refused and the choice is made for justice, radical love, and liberation, the power of death is overthrown. Resurrection is radical courage.

Resurrection means that death is overcome in those precise instances when human beings choose life, refusing the threat of death. Jesus climbed out of the grave in the Garden of Gethsemane when he refused to abandon his commitment to the truth even though his enemies threatened him with death. On Good Friday, the Resurrected One was Crucified.

NOTES

1. Perdita Huston, *Third World Women Speak Out* (New York: Frederick A. Praeger, 1979), 36.

2. Mary Daly, *Beyond God the Father* (Boston: Beacon Press, 1973), 77.

3. Gregory of Nyssa, *The Great Catechism*, chap. 24.

4. Matthew Fox, *Original Blessing* (Santa Fe: Bear & Co., 1983), 162.

5. Ibid., 159.

6. Ibid., 164.

7. Anselm, *Cur Deus Homo*, chap. 9.

8. Ibid., chap. 12.

9. Ibid., chap. 11.

10. Walter Rauschenbusch, *A Theology for the Social Gospel* (New York: Abingdon Press, 1917), 174, chap. 15.

11. Ibid., 49, chap. 6.

12. Ibid., 184, chap. 15.

13. From John Driver, *Understanding the Atonement for the Mission of the Church* (Scottdale, Pa.: Herald Press, 1986), 129–46.

14. Judy Grahn, "From Sacred Blood to the Curse and Beyond," in *The Politics of Women's Spirituality*, ed. Charlene Spretnak (Garden City, N.Y.: Anchor Books, 1982), 265–79.

15. Nancy Jay ("Sacrifice as Remedy for Having Been Born of Woman," in *Immaculate and Powerful*, ed. C. W. Atkinson, C. H. Buchanan, and M. R. Miles [Boston: Beacon Press, 1985], 283–309) shows the relationship between blood sacrifice and the subordination of women.

16. Mary Daly, *Gyn/Ecology* (Boston: Beacon Press, 1978), 82.

17. Alfred of Rievaulx, quoted by Caroline Walker Bynum in *Jesus as Mother* (Berkeley: University of California Press, 1982), 123.

18. William of St. Theirry, quoted by Bynum, *Jesus as Mother*, 120.

19. Peter Abelard, "Exposition of the Epistle to the Romans," in Gerhard O. Forde, "Caught in the Act: Reflections on the Work of Christ," in *Word and World*, vol. III, no. 1, p. 22.

20. Helmut Thielicke, *The Ethics of Sex*, trans. John W. Doberstein (New York: Harper & Row, 1964), 79–98.

21. Ibid., 88.

22. Ronald Goetz, "The Suffering God: The Rise of a New Orthodoxy," *The Christian Century* (April 16, 1986): 385.

23. Ibid.

24. Personalism is the name of any theory that makes personality the supreme philosophical principle; idealistic personalism makes persons (and selves) the only reality. E.g., Edgar Sheffield Brightman, *An Introduction to Philosophy* (New York: Holt & Co., 1951), 218.

25. Edgar Sheffield Brightman, *The Problem of God* (New York: Abingdon Press, 1930), 113.

26. Ibid.

27. Edgar Sheffield Brightman, *The Finding of God* (New York: Abingdon Press, 1931), 123.

28. Ibid., 140.

29. Brightman, *Problem of God*, 94.

30. Goetz, "Suffering God," 389.

31. Jurgen Moltmann, *The Crucified God* (New York: Harper & Row, 1974), 51.

32. Ibid.

33. Ibid.

34. Martin Luther King, Jr., quoted in *A Testament of Hope*, ed. James Washington (New York: Harper & Row, 1986), 47.

35. Quoted in *The Church Is All of You*, ed. James Brockman (Minneapolis: Winston Press, 1984), 94.

36. Ibid., 69.

37. Jon Sobrino, *Christology at the Crossroads* (Maryknoll, N.Y.: Orbis Books, 1978), 373.

38. Ibid., 224.

39. Sheila Collins, *A Different Heaven and Earth* (Valley Forge, Pa.: Judson Press, 1974), 88–89.

40. Sobrino, *Christology at the Crossroads*, 371.

41. Ibid.

42. William R. Jones, *Is God a White Racist?* (New York: Anchor Press, 1973), 81.

43. William R. Jones, "Reconciliation and Liberation in Black Theology: Some Implications for Religious Education," *Religious Education* 67 (Sept.–Oct. 1972): 386.

44. Jones, *Is God a White Racist?* 68.

45. Ibid., 55.

46. Ibid., 13.

47. Ibid., 29.

48. Ibid., 188.

49. Ibid., 201.

50. Ibid., 196.

51. Ibid., 202.

52. Remarks made by Jacqueline Grant in a panel discussion entitled, "Women's Issues in the Development of Black Religion," American Academy of Religion, Nov. 26, 1985.

53. Carter Heyward, *The Redemption of God* (Washington, D.C.: University Press of America, 1982), 54–57.

54. Ibid., 58.

55. Ibid., 168–69.

2

The Western Religious Tradition and Violence Against Women in the Home

ROSEMARY RADFORD RUETHER

Domestic violence against women—wife battering or beating—is rooted in and is the logical conclusion of basic patriarchal assumptions about women's subordinate status. Traditional patriarchal law denied women adults autonomous civil status. Women were treated legally as permanent minors and dependents of fathers and husbands. They had no right to represent themselves politically as legal persons. Their right to inherit and transmit property was also limited and their earnings were regarded as belonging to their husbands. Civilly, women were nonpersons who were represented by their male guardians, although the adult single woman and the widow had a somewhat anomalous status. The daughter or wife was in some sense property or chattel, regarded as being owned by her father or husband. Marriage was a business deal transacted between two males; the woman often had little say, at least legally. Women's legal status was assimilated into that of children and slaves as dependents and quasi property, as persons who had no right to assert their own will but who were bound under a yoke of obedience and servitude to their lords.[1] The term "lord" *(dominus)* was used simultaneously for God as Lord of the world, the aristocracy as masters of the lower classes, and finally the male head of household as lord of his wife, children, and servants. The oft-repeated metaphor, drawn from St. Paul, that the woman has no head of her own, but her husband is her head as she is his body, summed up the subjugated status of woman.[2]

The subordinate legal status of women was expressed in classical

Christianity in an elaborate theory of the inferiority of woman's nature. Scholastic theology borrowed Aristotelian biology. Aristotle taught that women were a secondary biological species. The male contributed the form of the child in procreation. The woman was only an incubator who grew the child in her body. Normatively, every male seed would produce a perfect image of its maker, namely, another male. But at times the lower material principle, represented by the mother, gained aberrant dominance over the higher principle of the father and a "misbegotten male," or female, was born. The female was by nature inferior in her capacity for thought, will, and physical activity.[3] Women were natural slaves and, like slaves, it was their nature to be obedient servants in all things to their heads and masters.[4]

Scholastic theology adopted this theory and defined women as misbegotten males who have, by nature, a defective capacity for humanity. Theologically, this was expressed by Augustine's theory that women in themselves lacked the "image of God." They could be said to reflect the image of God only when taken together with the male, their head. But men represent the image of God fully and completely in themselves.[5] Women also cannot represent Christ, who is perfect humanity. Therefore, only men can be priests and represent Christ in the Christian community, as well as headship in secular society.

To this theory of woman's defective nature in the order of creation Christian theology added the idea that she was disproportionately responsible for sin. The original Genesis stories suggest women's co-creation with man and their co-responsibility for sin. But in the New Testament the narrative is clearly biased against Eve. First Timothy 2:12–14 reads,

> I do not allow women to teach or to have authority over men. They must keep quiet. For Adam was created first and then Eve. And it was not Adam who was deceived. It was the woman who was deceived and broke God's law.

Traditional Christianity adopted this reading of the Fall story, in which Eve was the primary guilty partner in causing historic evil in the world. While Adam went along with her almost as an act of noblesse oblige, he was relatively innocent of any responsibility. Woman's subordinate status, therefore, not only reflects her original inferior nature but also is a just punishment for her guilt in causing evil to come into the world, thereby leading to the death of Christ. Far from saving her, the death of Christ only deepens her guilt, while it absolves the male of his fault and allows him to represent the male savior.

These theories of woman's inferiority are formulated in the work of the great master of scholastic theology, Thomas Aquinas. According to Aquinas, and following Aristotle's theory, woman is defective by nature, a "misbegotten male." Her subjugation, unlike that of the slave, existed even before sin because it belongs to the original order of nature as created by God. Therefore it follows that woman cannot represent Christ or be ordained because she cannot represent headship in society or the church.[6]

These theories were adapted during the Reformation. Martin Luther's version is slightly different. According to Luther, Eve was not inferior to Adam in the original creation; she was originally his equal. But because of her sin she was punished by God, demoted to a far inferior creature than she was originally, and she must suffer subjugation to the male as a punishment for her sin. In Luther's words:

> The wife was made subject to the man by the Law which was given after sin. . . . The rule remains with the husband and the wife is compelled to obey him by God's command. He rules the home and the state, wages war, defends his possessions, tills the soil, plants, builds, etc. The woman, on the other hand, is like a nail driven into the wall. She sits at home . . .[7]

Grumbling by women about this status or their efforts to change it represent for Luther a wrongheaded effort to revolt against a punishment that they must be forced to accept and bear as an expression of their sinful status. The story is no better for women when told by John Calvin. While Puritanism stressed spiritual as well as physical compatibility in marriage, this compatibility was something of a one-way street. It depended on the woman submitting her will to her lord in all things and he in turn caring for her. The order of compatibility was clearly hierarchical, not equalitarian. Puritans saw this hierarchical order of marriage and the family as the original order of creation, the order that should be restored in the Christian home.[8] Any woman who flaunted her will against male authority was sinful, disrupted the order of nature and society, and was very likely a witch.

JUSTIFICATION OF VIOLENCE

It is important to recognize that this theological "gangbanging" of women went beyond depriving them of legal rights and excluding them from higher education and professional and leadership roles in church and society. It also took the form of certain legal justifications of physical violence. It was then and still is generally assumed in the patriarchal family that parents have certain rights, including the right to beat their children, both girls and boys. Some patriarchal societies, such as those of ancient Rome and Islam, even gave the father the right to kill or sell his children.

The right to kill girl children has been exercised throughout history. Girl children, regarded as less valuable than boys, were often killed at birth. This occurred in the Middle Ages as well, although the church opposed all infanticide. It also justified the killing of daughters suspected of sexual improprieties.

The church also offered women the woman's community of the religious order, which at the time offered the only prospects for education and autonomous leadership roles for women in society. Furthermore, if a woman declared that she had a religious vocation, the church would defend her against all the demands of her family that she marry. In these areas the church offered some alleviation of the power of the patriarchal family over women.

But the church offered little help to women in the area of marriage. This was partly due to the hostility to marriage that characterized Christianity for much of its historic existence. Certainly from the third to the sixteenth centuries, marriage was regarded as an inferior vocation. The married woman was the epitome of the carnal Eve. Her subordination and need for punishment were fully stressed. The contempt of celibate legislators for married women may have some connection with the fact that there crept into church law justification of the right of husbands to beat their wives. It is significant that rabbinic law in the same period was much more solicitous of the psychological and physical well-being of the wife and allowed a woman to ask for divorce if her husband beat her.[9]

In the classical compilation of canon law made by Gratian in the twelfth century, it is said that a husband may chastise his wife but not beat her. The glosses on this text made by subsequent canon lawyers, however, interpreted it to mean that the husband might strike his wife in anger but not subject her to stripes under the whip like a slave.[10] A degree of the Council of Toledo in A.D. 400 decrees that if a wife of the clergy transgresses his commands, the husband may beat the wife, keep her bound in their house, and force her to fast but "not unto death." The principle also passed into canon law that the cleric has a right to beat his wife harder than does the ordinary man.[11] Most customary and town law in the medieval and Renaissance periods gave husbands the right to beat their wives, although it was usually said that they should do so "reasonably" or "moderately." For example, the town law of the city of Villefranche reads, "All the inhabitants of Villefranche have the right to beat their wives, so long as death does not ensue."[12]

The literature and advice books of the period deepen this impression that men are justified in using physical violence against their wives, who are always depicted as provoking or "asking for" such violence. In the *Book of the Knight of Tour-Landry,* for example, which sets forth the duties and usages of upper-class society, the story is told of a wife who rebukes her husband in public. He strikes her to the floor with his fist and breaks her nose with his foot, thereby giving her a permanent mark on her face. The book teaches this story as a "good lesson" for women of what they ought to expect if they cross their husbands in such a fashion.[13]

Thomas More gives us some of the most savage indications of the upper-class Renaissance man's ideas of wife punishment. He tells one story of a man who chops off his wife's head with an ax because she persists in scolding him. The prince of the area justifies the husband because it is agreed that the wife "asked for this" with her persistent scolding.[14] Puritan towns, among others, into the late seventeenth century decreed terrible punishments, such as the ducking stool or specially devised cages which held their mouths closed, for women accused by their husbands of being "scolds."[15] That this savage attitude reflects More's ideals is seen in his *Utopia,* in which he defines the ideal society. Husbands are pictured as chastising their wives, the wives as ministering to their husbands in all things, falling prostrate at their feet on holy days, and asking their forgiveness if they have offended them in any way.[16]

WITCHCRAFT AND HOSTILITY
TOWARD WOMEN

Perhaps the most important outbreak of hostility toward women was seen in the persecution of witchcraft. People today have a tendency to imagine that this occurred in the "Dark Ages" before the modern Enlightenment. But in the actual Dark Ages, the ninth to eleventh centuries, there was no persecution of witchcraft. Persecution of witches grew steadily in the late Middle Ages, the fourteenth and fifteenth centuries, and then subsided. It was revived and claimed its greatest number of victims from the mid-sixteenth to the end of the seventeenth centuries. Protestants and Catholics were equally enthusiastic about witch hunting. Puritan Massachusetts, indeed, was one of the last places to have a major witch-hunting outbreak, in the last decade of the seventeenth century.

Although not all victims of witchcraft persecution were women, overwhelmingly, women were targets. Moreover, the official image of the witch was female. In fact, witch hunting tended to stop when this image was violated and men of some social standing came to be accused.[17] Witch hunting flourished most when it kept to its stereotypic images of the marginal old woman living by herself or the "loose" young woman who was too free and independent with her sex and her tongue. In both cases marginal women, women who did not fall under "proper" male authority, women who talked back and led their lives independently, were most likely to be regarded as the town witches.

Herbal medicines, spells, and occult powers could be easily attributed to such women because the healing arts, that is, spells and midwifery, was an occupation open to women without other sources of economic support. The whole village depended on these healing women; but the women became victims when paranoia about witchcraft demanded scapegoats. Some scholars see the witchcraft persecutions of this period as either an effort to reduce an excess marginal female population or an effort by the rising medical profession to eliminate its popular rivals.[18]

Official witch-hunting manuals defined the witch as female and linked this definition with what were regarded as the female's naturally demonic nature, her greater tendencies to lust, and her inability to control her sinful disposition due to both her inferior moral nature and her greater corruption by sin. Since Christ was a male, the male also was more protected from demonic impulses than women. The classic witch-hunting manual *The Hammer of Witches*, written by two Dominican inquisitors in the fifteenth century, shows how the theories of female inferiority are linked with suspicions of witchcraft:

When a woman thinks alone, she thinks evil. . . . I have found a woman more bitter than death, and a good woman subject to carnal lust. They are more impressionable than men and more ready to receive the influence of the disembodied spirit. . . . They have slippery tongues. . . . Since they are weak, they find an easy and secret manner of vindicating themselves in witchcraft. They are feebler both in mind and body. It is not surprising that they should come more under the spell of witchcraft. As regards intellect or understanding of spiritual things, they seem to be of a different nature than men. . . . Women are intellectually like children. . . . And it should be noted that there was a defect in the formation of the first woman, since she was formed from the bent rib, the rib of the breast which is bent in the contrary direction to a man. . . . And since through the first defect in their intelligence, they are always more prone to abjure the faith, so through their second defect of inordinate passions, they search for, brood over and inflict various vengeances, either by witchcraft or some other means. Wherefore it is no wonder that so great a number of witches exist in this sex. . . . Women have weaker memories, and it is a natural vice in them not to be disciplined, but to follow their own impulses without any sense of what is due. . . . She is a liar by nature. . . . Let us consider her gait, posture and habit, in which she is vanity of vanities. . . . Woman is a wheedling and secret enemy. For the sake of fulfilling their lusts they consort even with devils.[19]

Many of the methods of investigating witchcraft put women in a no-win situation. Women were stripped and shaved, and any blemish on their bodies was pricked. All abnormalities were regarded as witch's teats, proof positive of witchcraft. Women were subjected to torture. If they held out and refused to confess, it was assumed that they must be witches, since a woman's inferior physical nature would not allow her to withstand torture unless she was receiving help from the devil. Women were tied and thrown in ponds. If they floated, they were convicted of witchcraft, but if they sank, they were exonerated, since it was believed that water would expel a witch. Either way, they were unlikely to survive the test.

We can see from these examples that historical Christianity defined women as inferior, subordinate, and prone to the demonic. These images justified almost limitless violence against them whenever they crossed the male will at home or in society. Woman as victim is the underside of patriarchal history, seldom given respect or concern from agents of morality or law enforcement. Women particularly have been subjected to the double bind of blaming the victim in innumerable and convoluted ways that women even today have a difficult time refuting.

The assumption of patriarchal society is that when women are victims of either verbal abuse or physical violence, ranging from beating to rape, they themselves are responsible for it. They have "asked for it" and therefore can receive no sympathy, compensation, or restraint of their violators, but only insult added to injury.

REPRODUCTIVE RIGHTS

Besides physical violence and legal and cultural suppression, there is another important area where patriarchal society and patriarchal religion have cooperated in the subjugation of women: the right of women to control their own reproductive power. It is often imagined that contraceptives and safe abortion have become possible only through modern medicine. Women could not possibly be liberated and freed to join in other occupations as long as biology and the medical ignorance of society made women subject to continual births throughout their adult lives (most women did not live beyond menopause until recently).

This concept is deceptive. In fact, primitive people often had safe and reliable herbal contraceptives and abortifacients. We might remember that the modern contraceptive pill was discovered by a researcher who went to remote Mexican villages to find the roots traditionally used by Indian women as contraceptives, brought these back, and synthesized them in his laboratory. It is not primitive ignorance but patriarchal ideology that decrees that women should not use contraceptives or seek abortion and should accept whatever pregnancies "God" and males impose on them.

One of the primordial roots of the male need to subjugate women may be that women biologically play a predominant role in birth. The male contribution is quickly over, and then the woman is in possession of the child. She becomes absorbed in growing it in her body and then suckling it, and loses interest in the male. The male cannot be sure that the child she produces is actually his. Women seem to be the center of the world of birth. This experience was doubtless the root of the early image of the divine as a mother goddess.

As patriarchal systems of power have developed, one of their fundamental expressions has been the assertion of control over women's procreative power. Women's chastity before and in marriage has been rigidly regulated, in contrast to the sexual freedom allowed males, in order to assure the paternity of the child. Women's ability to make decisions about conceiving or bearing a child are sternly curtailed, since this should be a male, not a female, prerogative. From an early period the church intervened to denounce as immoral, and to banish knowledge about, contraception and abortion that had been widespread in antiquity. Traditionally, Christianity has asserted that it is gravely sinful for the woman to try to control reproduction. In this area especially she must be totally resigned to the outside forces that control her, forces referred to in impersonal cosmic terms, such as biological destiny and divine will—as though they were forces beyond human control.

Christianity even disliked the idea that a woman should have a say in whether or not to accept the sexual demands of her husband. Her sexuality was defined in canon law and moral theology as the "debt of her body" which she owes her husband in the marriage contract. She is bound to serve him sexually, on demand, no matter what her own physical disposition might be. The male control of the right of divorce is also a part of this system of male control over women as wives and reproducers.

In modern times, Christian churches, Protestant as well as Catholic, have become primary agents in the crusade against contraception and abortion. Laws in many states making contraceptive knowledge a crime were passed by puritanical Protestants in the late nineteenth century, not by Roman Catholics. Today, however, the Catholic church has taken the lead in the crusade against women's control over their own bodies. It is anxious to promote this as an ecumenical endeavor and has succeeded in forming a coalition with traditionalist Protestant and Jewish groups as well.

The "Right to Life" campaign focuses on the bloody fetus, which is usually imaged as an almost full-grown infant. But the very name by which this group refers to itself—Right to Life—is misleading, since these groups have very little concern for "life" in the broader sense. They happily support capital punishment and war, and they show little interest in the economic survival of children after birth. Moreover, they do not promote the rational alternative to abortion, which is cheap and accessible clinics where contraceptive information and devices may be obtained. Few women would choose abortion, after all, over preventable pregnancy. The Catholic crusade particularly still hides, in its attack on abortion, a rejection of contraception as well. Thus the Right to Life movement must be seen primarily as a reaction to female autonomy, whose aim is to control the center of patriarchal power over women, namely, their control over their wombs.

CONCLUSION

Although women's legal, professional, educational, and medical emancipation have grown greatly in the last century, many of these gains are not assured. The powers of reaction also grow as women attempt to further their emancipation. In particular, we must see the reaction against a woman's right to control her reproductive powers as closely linked with reactionary movements (e.g., the "Total Woman" movement) that seek to reassert the full patriarchal theory of woman's total subordination to the male will.[20] Conservative religion is the chief promoter of these movements, which often meet in churches. Moreover, the ideology behind the total woman movement always contains a great deal of biblical and theological sanctification. Women's subordination again is seen as the order of nature. The hierarchy of Christ over the church and the maleness of God are seen as the ultimate sanction of hierarchical society.

These reactionary movements teach that subordination is God's will and the root of true human happiness for women as well as men. Only as women give up their sinful desires for equality and self-definition and resign themselves totally to their husbands' slightest demands, no matter how unreasonable or peremptory, can peace and happiness be restored to the family. At a time of widespread chaos in society and the family, when many women do not really feel equipped for the tasks of equality, these falsely simple answers have widespread appeal to women.

Christianity has in it the seeds of an alternative theory, a theory of liberation, equality, and dignity for all persons. But this idea has seldom been applied to women in the religious tradition, either historically or today. Instead the church has been preponderantly on the side of theories of women's subjugation. It is no accident that the religious heirs of this conservative tradition are prime agents of antiliberation reaction in American society today.

NOTES

1. English common law in the seventeenth century defined the married woman as a *femme coverte* who lost all civil identity of her own. See *The Lawes Provision for Women* (London, 1632), 124–25.

2. Paul, 1 Cor. 11:3; Eph. 5:22–28.

3. Aristotle, *On the Generation of Animals* 1.729b; 2.731b, 737a, 738b.

4. Aristotle, *Politics* 1.1–2.

5. Augustine, *De Trinitate* 7.7.10.

6. Aquinas, *Summa Theologica*, Pt. 1. Q. 92, "On the Production of Woman"; Pt. 3, Q. 39, Ar. 1, "Whether the Female Sex Is an Impediment to Receiving Orders."

7. Luther, *Lectures on Genesis*, 2:23; 3:16.

8. See Elizabeth Clark and Herbert Richardson, "The Puritan Transformation of Marriage," in *Women and Religion* (New York: Harper & Row, 1977), 144–45.

9. L. Finkelstein, *Jewish Self-Government in the Middle Ages* (1924), 217.

10. G. G. Coulton, "Woman's Life," in *Medieval Panorama* (New York: Cambridge University Press, 1939), 615.

11. Ibid.

12. Ibid., 617.

13. Ibid.

14. Thomas More, *English Works*, 1187. From G. G. Coulton, *Life in the Middle Ages* (New York: Cambridge University Press, 1931), vol. 3:165–67.

15. Gags and ducking stools were among the prescribed punishment for "scolds." See Roger Thompson, *Women in Stuart England and America* (London: Routledge & Kegan Paul, 1974), 10.

16. Thomas More, *Utopia*, ed. Edward Surtz (New Haven: Yale University Press, 1964), 77, 143.

17. See H. C. E. Midelfort, *Witch Hunting in South West Germany, 1563–84* (Stanford, Calif.: Stanford University Press, 1972), chaps. 6, 7. See also Marion L. Starkey, *The Devil in Massachusetts* (New York: Alfred A. Knopf, 1949), passim.

18. The demographic thesis of excess female population in the seventeenth century is explored in Alan McFarlane, *Witchcraft in Tudor and Stuart England* (London: Routledge & Kegan Paul, 1970). Rivalry with professionally credentialed medical personnel is explored in Barbara Ehrenreich and Deirdre English, *Witches, Midwives and Nurses* (New York: Feminist Press, 1973).

19. *Malleus Maleficarum*, trans. Montague Summers (London: J. Rodker, 1928), Pt. I, sec. 6.

20. See, e.g., Helen Andelin, *Fascinating Womanhood* (Santa Barbara, Calif.: Pacific Press, 1971); and Marabel Morgan, *The Total Woman* (Old Tappan, N.J.: Revell, 1973).

3

And A Little Child Will Lead Us: Christology and Child Abuse

RITA NAKASHIMA BROCK

Until this century, parental treatment of children, short of murder, was considered a private matter, the proper domain of the home in which women did the primary work. Few theologians have examined the underlying structures of child abuse in religious doctrines. I believe that this is so partly because child rearing, as the responsibility largely of women, has not been regarded as a serious theological topic. Hence, the subject of children as a religious issue was placed under the less prestigious area of Christian education. I propose to examine here the theological implications of our having ignored children as a theological subject.

Child abuse is the result of many complicated problems. If we are to protect our children, we must examine all the issues surrounding abuse, rather than just blame parents. I believe that patriarchy is the encompassing social system that sanctions child abuse. Theologically, the patriarchal family has been and continues to be a cornerstone for christological doctrines, especially in father-son imagery and in the unquestioned acceptance of benign paternalism as the norm for divine power. The following feminist analysis will examine the implicit structure of parent-child relationships in patriarchal families and the problems with theological doctrines based on the social structures of a patriarchal society. I will conclude this examination with a few suggestions for understanding Christ without reinforcing the destructive patterns of the patriarchal family and its power systems.

Patriarchy, which is neither inevitable nor universal, has emerged

42

through a complex process. Charlotte B. O'Kelly and Larry S. Carney claim that a series of factors in agrarian and pastoral societies led to male dominance and the formation of patriarchy. These factors include the development of the value of possessions, either land or animals, a hostile environment with scarce resources, and, most important, warfare. The shift away from the social organization of many foraging societies, which are characterized by cooperation, egalitarianism, flexibility in human relationships, extensive kinship systems, social stability, and individual integrity and freedom, is a shift toward male dominance and more hostile and insecure selves. With the rise of male dominance and warfare, the structure of kinship focused on the patriarchal family, with a shift toward control-oriented parenting, socialized gender differences, and separate societal roles and spheres of operation.[1]

This basic social structure of the patriarchal family, a structure that socializes women for domestic responsibility and men for dominance and aggression in public arenas, represents an important element in Christian theology. Christological doctrines use analogies to the patriarchal family to articulate the meaning of Christ. These doctrines assume the unquestioned norm of the patriarchal family. Hence, I believe such christological doctrines reflect views of divine power that sanction child abuse on a cosmic scale and sustain benign paternalism.[2] In justifying this assertion about child abuse and Christology, I will begin with the self-identities produced by the patriarchal family, discuss the implications for how such people in our male-dominated society understand relationships, show the connection to Christology, and propose an alternative way to understand divine incarnation.

SELF-IDENTITY

Our definition of ourselves is crucial to both our understanding of relationships and the restructuring of our religious ideas, which are under feminist attack as androcentric. A number of recent feminist works have analyzed the impact of sex-role stereotyping and the allocation of tasks by gender on our culture's views of self. Many feminist gender-based analyses of self-identity assert that divergent views of the self occur in males and females. This current feminist shift in focus from views of equality characteristic of the 1970s to an examination of the value of the difference women's socialization brings to our species has emerged with the critical mass of women required to develop a new intellectual consciousness. While most feminists who examine uniquely female ways of seeing tend to assert that differences in gender identity are socially produced, we believe the differences are important for understanding androcentrism and male dominance.[3] Much of the data used to indicate the differences is not new, but the interpretation and valuation of the differences are.

In *The Reproduction of Mothering: Psychoanalysis and the Sociology of Gender*, Nancy Chodorow characterizes the masculine self, a product of Western industrialized capitalist society, as sharply ego-identified and oriented toward goals, tasks, and rules. Male identity is based on differentiation from others, on generalized, abstract masculine roles, and on the rejection of femininity and denial of affective relation. The male sees himself as (1) needing to remain apart from relationships and affiliation; (2) proven by success in competitive contexts, and (3) reaching maturation through achievement of autonomy in the public sphere. That is, he becomes the good warrior and protector.

The feminine self is characterized by Chodorow as highly focused on affiliation and affective relationships, an orientation important to nurturing life in the domestic sphere. Females develop a sense of identity by connecting to others and remain more particularistic and context-oriented. The female feels herself incomplete without a complex of relationships of differing kinds. The female avoids open conflict and competition and feels herself confirmed in the capacity to nurture others. That is, she becomes the good warrior's protectee, servant, nurse, and breeder.

Chodorow concludes that sex-role stereotyping in the patriarchal family structures of our culture reproduces the two views of self. She asserts that extremely divergent and neurotic forms of masculine and feminine identity occur when the primary caretaker of children is control-oriented. Neurotic masculine identity is brittle, isolated, and afraid of relatedness, associating intimacy with violence; it wants the domination and control of others and uses a rigid and punitive superego to control itself and others; and it is rebellious, especially against anything feminine. Neurotic feminine identity lacks any separate sense of self; it is formed by the demands of others, especially by the superego structures of another; it perceives itself as victim; it is dependent upon external relationships; and will use inappropriate others, such as children, to fill the consuming emotional needs of an insecure ego.

Views of power are closely linked to stereotyped masculine and feminine self-identities. Power is how the self feels itself present, alive, and sustained in the world. The possession and use of power is yoked to self-esteem and self-protection. David McClelland notes that the male experiences power as something he gains, drawing more and more to himself and using the acquired power to gain more over against others who threaten his power.[4] Involvement with others is tied to a qualification of power and identity. Strength is the ability to control things external to the self. This view of power is inherently competitive and hierarchical, essential to capitalism and the nuclear arms race.

McClelland found a different experience of power in traditional females, one based in their childrearing roles. Feminine power involves the need to nurture others. In giving of herself to others to facilitate and empower their growth, the female feels powerful. Hence the feminine view of power is grounded in generosity, empathy, yielding, and relinquishment.

Both masculine and feminine selves see possessing power, in each of their distinctive forms, as essential to self-worth. In a system of dominance and submission these two views of power require each other. The feminine view of power does not interfere with the masculine need to dominate; exploiter male and exploited female go hand in hand. A deep unrest stirs in such a polarized system of identity and power. Chodorow believes the system contains its own implosive self-destruction because the system produces unhappy, unstable selves who use power to exploit others.

Both gender-linked views of self and power, especially in extreme form, are fraught with difficulties. Even as it uses the reality of women's experience as a resource, the feminist solution must go further than a gender-based concept. Research on crosscultural gender roles and on people who cross gender lines in our culture indicates that few gender-linked traits are biologically inevitable. Our society's hope and our planet's survival lie in our capacity to free ourselves from rigid gender roles, especially as they feed structures of dominance and submission.[5] Feminist analyses of gender-based identity have been an important critical tool for examining the extent to which androcentrism has been the dominant bias of Western thought. In addition, such analysis has helped us see what alternatives women provide for understanding relationships.

Most feminists would assert that all human beings are relational beings. We are, therefore, profoundly connected to one another, an important insight that androcentrism has tended to obscure. This insight is gained from women's role in the early formative stages of self-formation and from feminist reflection upon our adult life together. Hence, this discussion of self begins with the assumption that relationship is essential to self.[6]

An important distinction must be drawn, however, between the intimacy of relationship and the fusion of parent-child relationships under patriarchy. Alice Miller, a Swiss object-relations therapist, contends that virtually all childrearing in our culture is control oriented.[7] The use of control takes away a child's sense of distinct identity and subsumes it as an extension of parental will. Whether parents use techniques such as positive reinforcement or physical abuse, the parents shape the child into a being who reflects the parent's needs or wishes. Miller believes that all children need care—protection, security, touching, tenderness, and emotional connection—and that they have a right to express their needs and have them respected. The use of control and punishment of any sort abuses children, producing lifelong damaging effects. Children learn to bury their own feelings and needs, to rely on false selves that mirror their parents' feelings and needs, and to respect the powers of authority and dominance, rather than their own feelings and needs. Without direct access to one's feelings and the ability to express them, intimacy is impossible.

Miller's description of parenting fits the picture, given in O'Kelly and Carney, of the shift away from the care-oriented childrearing of foraging societies to the more repressive, controlling practices of horticultural, pastoral, and agrarian societies, which have become the dominant global forms of social organization. If we align Miller's analysis of false selves with Chodorow's analysis of masculine and feminine identity, we can begin to see that both gender-linked views of self are false.[8] Both the male who invests himself in goals, competition, and control and the female self that relies upon dependency, approval, and nurturing others rest their self-worth upon the world outside themselves. Their sense of worth lies in the denial of their own subjectivity, leading to the denial of their own feelings and needs. Hence, their true selves are replaced by false selves that exploit or are exploited by the world, and they seek ways to meet their needs for self-esteem through their reenactment of early parent-child patterns in which they have lost their capacity for intimacy.

While Miller does not focus her work on gender difference, her claims about control, combined with Chodorow's thesis about the creation of gender difference, imply that one of the main factors that create sharp gender differences in our culture is the rearing of children by persons, primarily mothers, who seek to use children to meet adult needs or who seek to control children. For many women in Western culture little beyond domestic work is available to meet the adult human need for creativity and fulfilling, productive work. In addition, the social power structures of male dominance make the control of those less powerful a norm in human interactions.

Rather than creating confident selves capable of intimacy, childrearing in male-dominated Western culture causes the fusion of selves. Harriett Coldhor Lerner[9] points out that in early relationships in which family members are too fused and parents are unable to see their children as separate from themselves several reactions ensue. People will believe others "cause" their behavior and will be unable to see their reactions as their own. Since such relationships are emotionally highly charged, a child may react by rebellion and pushing away. These reactions maintain fusion because both parties continue to see each other's behavior and reactions as "caused" by the other. If, on the other hand, a child reacts by remaining dependent, the fusion causes a child to feel guilty and therefore negatively about itself if it makes any attempt to separate, assert itself, or get angry. Selves in such families are confused.

The underlying difficulty in confused relationships, either in provoking reactions of rebellion and separation (angry or bossy response) or in reactions of dependency and need (helpless or depressive response), is that neither reaction produces selves who recognize true intimacy or respect the separateness and difference of others. Hence males who seek dominance and females who are compliant and dependent are not capable of much intimacy.

Fused relationships begin in the patriarchal family, but once the orientation is internalized, extend themselves into social systems. Parents who have been denied their selves in childhood and have not reclaimed them as adults have not had their need for love and respect met. As Chodorow also contends, such parents will use their children for their own needs. Miller states that rather than welcoming the child as a separate being with its own needs, requiring love and gentle respect, parents will see the child as someone who can be shaped to love them as they want to be loved or as someone who can be molded into the person they have always wanted to be, thereby protecting themselves from their own sense of failure. The parents will often treat the child in what they believe are loving ways, "stoning it with kisses," as Miller says, or using positive reinforcement. These benign forms of control still focus authority and truth in the parent. A child is expected to obey the will of a benign parent because that parent knows best. However, the primary orientation toward the child is still one of control.

Not even in the practice of benign parenting is the child seen as the source of wisdom for the parent. Miller believes this attitude of control is grounded in a long history of using children to meet adult needs such as compensation for feelings of inferiority, a receptacle for unwanted feelings, an opportunity to exercise power, or a way to obtain pleasure that should be gotten from adults. Hence, children become victims of the parents' false selves.

If the parents of a child are control oriented in a more punitive and violent way, the consequences for the child's self-identity are far more devastating. Miller contends that all punishment used by parents chips away at the child's true self by shutting down its capacity to feel. The humiliation of children through abuse has been regarded as the means to shape children "for their own good." But such methods produce intense pain and suffering. Without someone to confirm feelings of suffering from the humiliation of punishment, children must bury their pain, for children cannot integrate experiences alone.

As adults, such children will split off their own pain and project it upon others by punishing their own children or by victimizing others weaker than themselves, a pattern that parallels masculine gender identity. As long as the pain remains buried, the person will be unable to empathize with another's pain or identify with victims of oppression. More typical of feminine gender identity is the tendency to seek sources outside the self that repeat the abusive punishments of childhood. Whether the reenactment of abuse is inflicted upon others or the self, the adult will blame the abuse on the abused.

One of the most devastating combinations of elements in childrearing described by Miller is the loving-punitive parent. The child receives both painful punishment and loving support from the same parent. In doing so, the child links the two together, confusing abuse with love. As an adult, a child so reared will be unable to accept or give a healthy, nondestructive love. Miller describes the emotional bonds of abusive love as more compelling than true intimacy unless the self is able to differentiate the two.

The false self produced by dominance and abuse is a self that rests its self-esteem in winning approval from significant others by empathetic union and/or success and achievement. In either case, the false self is held together by its ability to use others and the external world. The false self has lost the capacity to feel intense passions, and so is haunted by depression. It will idealize its parents and past, place blame for abuse on victims, and be unable to recognize healthy intimacy. Finally, the false self will seek to reproduce itself in others over whom it has control. All attempts to manage, change, and control a child produce a false self in the child. This thesis is Miller's most radical, for it demonstrates the fundamental relationship between the false self and power as the need for dominance, even when that dominance is benign.

Miller points out that well-meaning parents use control to train their children. They employ techniques such as deprivation of food or solitary confinement, entrapment, manipulation, emotional isolation, humiliation, embarrassment, cruelty, and physical pain. These techniques are supposed to teach a child love, respect for others, honesty, kindness, a love of truth, and the value of nonviolence. With such contradictory messages, *the only clear lesson is the value of power and authority.* The child learns that status and degree of power-over determine whether actions are judged good or bad. Hence, the more controlling and punishing the parent, the more the child will "behave" only when it fears a higher, punitive authority, and the more an adult so raised will seek power as a means of self-protection and as an opportunity to dominate others. In addition, the adult will protect authority from criticism, educate all those under his or her control to respect authority, and expect to sacrifice him or herself to higher authority. Again, as in the earlier analysis of gender-linked power, this system is immediately power as power-over. Exploiter and exploited require each other.

Power as dominance manifests itself in interpersonal and intrapersonal dimensions. Miller believes the false self behaves well by self-control over internal feelings that conflict with "right" behavior. Thus, the false self denies the subjectivity of the true self, using volition to suppress and control feeling. The false self uses its will to oppress the true self.

In a world that respects relationship rather than authority, Miller envisions that the rights of children will be respected and that we will begin to learn from them.

> Theoretically, I can imagine that someday we will regard our children not as creatures to manipulate or to change but rather as messengers from a world we once deeply knew, but which we have long since forgotten, who can reveal to us more about the true secrets of life, and also our own lives, than our parents were ever able to. We do not need to be told whether to be strict or permissive with our children. What we do need is to have respect for their needs, their feelings, and their individuality, as well as for our own.[10]

The abilities to act in and through love, to be nonviolent, to be generous, and to respect the rights and needs of others come from having been generously and gently loved and respected. Hence, the matrix of our connectedness is ambivalently powerful and yet essential to us. Our earliest relationships can steal our true selves or mirror them back to us. Without our true selves, morality is grounded in power, not love. This grounding in power as dominance and respect for authority characterizes much of Christian theology.

CHRISTOLOGY

Miller's psychological insights show how the false self needs to respect and protect a nostalgic image of the punitive rights or authority of the dominant parent, a common picture of the divine father. Mary Daly's landmark work *Beyond God the Father* levels clear and compelling charges against the use of masculine images for deity in a male-dominated culture. Criticisms of the patriarchal father image are presented by Charles Hartshorne, who criticizes the alienating nature of parental imagery and the contradiction between worshiping omnipotence and affirming love.[11] Other critics, such as Friedrich Nietzsche, Erich Fromm, and Ludwig Feuerbach, have leveled severe criticism at god the father. None, however, has explicitly articulated the relation of the image to child abuse.

While I do not wish to continue the use of the image of god the father, I think the longing in the use of the image needs to be understood because it has been such a powerful and complex metaphor. The very absence of an unconditionally loving and nurturing father in patriarchal society, the need for such love, and the presence of a punitive or distant father in the face of such needs, combined with the inability of mothers to meet all the needs of children, produce identification with the powerful father as a move toward self-protection, even as children still need love, as Miller and Chodorow contend. In a patriarchal culture, the theology of abused children who need love would, I think, be couched in terms of blame, guilt, and freedom from punishment through love from the father. Such a system requires the projection of any ambivalence onto an outside force or group and the rejection of those who might call the system into question. Alternatively, the longing for parental love might be articulated in the image of a benignly paternalistic father who is not at all punitive and loves all creation unconditionally, yet who is all powerful in control and authority.

If we base an entire theological system either on a human longing for an unreal past or in hierarchical authority, we have a system based in nostalgia, the nostalgia of dominated and abused children, an abuse epidemic in patriarchal culture. A nostalgic system prohibits honesty. Those persons, such as the humanists, psychoanalysts, and feminists I cited above, who seek to be honest about their life experiences in a patriarchal society, will be most alienated from and most likely to see through the destructive and nostalgic elements of the theological system. The honesty of their insights challenges the very structures of the society. As Muriel Rukeyser wrote, "What would happen if one woman told the truth about her life? The world would split open."[12]

Classical trinitarian formulas confuse parent and child and husband and wife, such that the father and son, or husband and wife, become one person and such that the father is seen to live some aspect of his own life in his son. Such confusion reflects male-dominant values in which all subordinates to the reigning patriarch are considered extensions of his identity. The confusion, which leads to fusion, is then repeated in the hierarchical bridegroom-bride images of Christ and church. The circularity, abstractness, and incoherence of trinitarian doctrines indicate to me that they tend to reinforce a sense of fusion, which is part of human experience, but which cannot satisfy finally our deepest spiritual needs for images of intimacy. Real intimacy can be grounded only in the contextual, unique, and particular, and in self-awareness. And intimacy is virtually impossible in systems of dominance and abuse.

As an aspect of trinitarian thought, Christology is often based in implicit elements of child abuse. Jesus, in his human aspect, is sacri-

51

ficed as the one perfect child. His sacrifice upholds the righteousness of the father who otherwise would require obedience from his incapable, sinful children. We are, it is asserted, born with a tragic flaw, and therefore must depend upon the perfect father and other persons with authority to reveal the truth. The punishment earned by us all is inflicted on the one perfect child. Then the father can forgive his wayward creation and love it. The doctrinal dependence upon patriarchal gender systems becomes clear when god as mother is substituted for father. The doctrines are not only virtually incomprehensible, the very suggestion of such substitutions raises enormous negative emotional reactions.

In Christology's more benignly paternalistic forms, the father, who loves all creation, does not desire to punish us. Instead, the father allows the son to suffer the consequences of the evil created by his wayward creation. The father stands by in passive anguish as his most beloved son is killed because the father refuses to interfere, even though he has the latent power to do so. The sacrifice of this perfect son is the way to new life with god the father. The death of the child and the intervention of the father after the punishment is inflicted, through the resurrection, are celebrated as salvific.

Christologies also use androcentric models that parallel warrior-hero images to describe Jesus as self-made through his own efforts, unsullied by assistance from sinful human beings. Jesus is someone who no longer is a member of his time and culture. He is fused into the deity whose will he is reenacting. Hence, Jesus, as the son of his divine father, is more perfect when his will is identical with his father's.

Such doctrines of salvation reflect and support images of benign paternalism, the neglect of children, or, at their worst, child abuse, making such behaviors acceptable as divine behavior—cosmic paternalism, neglect, and child abuse as it were.[13] The father allows, or even inflicts, the death of his only son. The goodness and power of the father and the unworthiness and powerlessness of his children make the father's punishment just and the blame the children's. The loving father's neglect is justified as protecting the freedom of humanity. Theology has tended to protect the authority, omnipotence, and omniscience of the father by justifying suffering as deserved or allowed.

While atonement Christologies emphasize God's grace and forgiveness, making it seem as if God accepts all persons whole without the demand that they be good and free of sin, such acceptance is contingent upon the abuse of the one perfect child. The experience of grace is lodged here, I believe, in a sense of relief at being relieved of punishment for one's inevitable failings and not in a clear sense of personal worth gained from an awareness of the unconditional nature of love. The shadow of the punitive father must always lurk behind atonement. He haunts images of forgiving grace. Benign paternalism functions by allowing a select group to be in a favored relationship with those in power, in this case with God, but the overall destructiveness of oppressive systems is not challenged by such benevolence. Hence, judgment on the unsaved is a necessary component of atonement.

As Miller points out, the tendency to accept blame for being wrong is characteristic of an abused child. The image of an ideal parent is projected onto a figure who is always right and who is the source of both love and righteous punishment. The projection helps the child manage its sense of rage about being hurt and made wrong. Such projection also usually leads to a need to split off the frightening or negative aspects of the self and project them onto others, as Christian theology has tended to do to women, Jews, and all "unsaved" others who are ready scapegoats.

Given the problematic nature of most christological doctrines, the task of reconstructing our understanding of the meaning of the center of Christianity is formidable. I believe, however, that it can be done. The task begins with the remembrance of a passionate, open, gentle self that feels the full range of human emotions and needs.

Remembrance of self means finding the damaged child inside all of us, the child that was once born whole, full of the grace of loving and needing love. Such a discovery leads us into anger and then grief about our pain, empathy that wells up from self-knowledge, passion that connects our anger to love, and joy in the freedom to love ourselves and others fully. The remembrance brings personal power and worth, power grounded in the capacity to connect with others as a self-aware, self-accepting person. The discovery carries ambivalence, however, for we become aware of how fragile we are. But our strength can come from that awareness of fragility, for only in recognizing it can we reach a healing and transforming self-awareness.

Remembrance of ourselves requires a loving person who helps us search, who is not afraid of the painfulness of the search, and who can mirror back our deeply rediscovered selves. Feminist sisterhood has been, in its best forms, a community of persons who touch each other through remembering the pain and ambivalence in our lives, claiming and feeling our anger, reconnecting to our bodies, and affirming sensuality and passion. The telling of truth about our lives in the midst of a community that cherishes that truth is the power of consciousness-raising that birthed this second feminist wave.[14]

In claiming our lost selves, we gain the self-acceptance crushed by patriarchy. To act out of our self-awareness does not mean conquering our self's urges and gaining self-control or surrendering our destiny to the control of others. To act well we must be willing to listen to our deepest needs and feelings and to transform self and world through the healing energies of an honest and dangerous memory that empowers us to give and receive love. Through that healing energy we may choose, in solidarity with those who suffer, to give ourselves to their struggle, but that solidarity, when it emerges from our self-awareness, is not an act of self-sacrifice, but of self-possession and connection to others.

We are most transformed, however, not by abstract ideas and theories, but by the living presence of others and by concrete images of transformation that allow us to claim our deepest feelings. Nelle Morton, in "The Goddess as Metaphoric Image," discusses the central importance of vivid, personal images that lead us through the ambivalence of our lives toward a vision of integrated wholeness.[15] Morton describes a waking vision she has of her dead mother, who apologizes to her for teaching her negative things about her body. In that apology her mother appeals to Morton to embrace and love her own distinctive body in all its life-giving ambivalence. Through an image that includes her own particular past pain and her present dis-ease, Morton is guided by her vision of her mother and of the goddess toward a transformation of her pain. She begins to embrace the brokenness of her body as a healing, energizing life force. Her vision is a wild and dangerous memory that brings her peace and self-acceptance.

It is essential that our religious ideas and images function to heal and empower us, rather than reinforce the dynamics of self-denial, self-hate, child abuse, and oppression. Through ideas and images that affirm the remembrance of ourselves we are led out of patriarchal theology. To heal ourselves and to liberate a suffering world, Christianity must find a healing image that leads us to dangerous, empowering memory and a theology grounded in such concrete memory.

CHRIST AS INCARNATE CHILD

For remembrance, I propose that we begin thinking of the Child as a divine image. In the image of the Child, we can see the grace born to us as the gift of the divine image mirrored in our being. And even in the midst of our wounds and our capacity to hurt others, we can see all persons as carrying that divine image. For no matter what our age, our Child never leaves us. The image is inclusive and conveys the fragility and strength of love of self and others. In understanding the divine spirit as Child incarnate in us, we can see the need to remain connected to the original grace of our playful, feeling self and to seek that self in others as divine incarnation. Imaging deity as Child locates divine power not in control and authority but in vulnerability, joy, openness, and interdependence. The Child compels us to identify with victims, with those who suffer, rather than with the powerful.

If we use the Child as a heuristic tool to examine the Gospel texts, the obvious passages about becoming like a Child to enter the *basileia* leap out, as do the birth narratives. But I wish to turn to less obvious images in which the vulnerability and interdependence of adults reveal the divine presence. Those adult images begin in the activity of healing and exorcism, in which the divine presence is brought to awareness not, as the texts tend to claim, by the presence of God in Jesus, but through the appearance of woundedness and oppression. The possessed, sick, oppressed, imprisoned, lame, and outcast reveal the presence of the fragility of the Child in us all. The healings and exorcisms reveal the redemptive nature of relationships in which woundedness—vulnerability—is claimed. There, in the event, is the divine spirit, not in a single person, but in the connections, in interdependence. My examination of images will focus first on the story of the hemorrhaging woman and then on the passion narrative.

In healing, the function of the healer is not to gain power but to share it. In the sharing process, woundedness reveals the sacred. Between healer and sufferer, an inequality of power exists that denies the afflicted the capacity to become whole. Hence, the flow of power between healer and afflicted represents the balancing of power inequities and the emergence of wholeness. This flow takes on a strong social dimension in Elisabeth Schüssler Fiorenza's interpretation of the story of the hemorrhaging woman, a woman with a flow of blood.[16]

The story, according to Schüssler Fiorenza, represents a social reality still experienced by women. In her study of the origins of patriarchy, Gerda Lerner argues convincingly that the roots of male dominance are in the reification, possession, and control of female sexuality and reproduction. Women's reproductive capacities become support for patriarchy, which uses subordination, rape, and murder to control women's sexual activity and usurps female birthing into male images of creation, ritual bleeding, and birthing. Lerner, along with O'Kelly and Carney, holds that systems of male dominance teach negative attitudes about women's bodies: their bleeding is polluting, their birthing is problematic, and their genitals are dirty.[17]

With these sexist attitudes toward women's bodies commonly acknowledged, the healing stories of the hemorrhaging woman and Jairus's daughter demonstrate a vision of what life in the *basileia* could be for women, according to Schüssler Fiorenza. The healing of the woman with hemorrhages is placed between the beginning and end of the healing of Jairus's daughter (Mark 5:21–43). The reasons for the two females' ailments are not given. Schüssler Fiorenza notes that the juxtaposition of the two stories creates interlocking meanings. Both females were afflicted with crises associated with the status of women in Greco-Roman and Hebraic society. The adult woman was sick with one of the most polluting signs of female adulthood. The adolescent was on the threshold of a similar curse, puberty. The woman had suffered with a flow of blood for exactly the same period of time as it had taken Jairus's daughter to reach the official age of puberty and marriageability.

The woman's hemorrhage was the affliction of adult women in magnified form. She suffered from her very femaleness. The subjective perspective of the woman is unusually vivid in the narrative. Her hope is evident in the report of her thoughts. Her fear is depicted in her confession to her deed. Her faith and courage reestablish her wholeness. Her courage comes from knowing vulnerability and, despite her fear, reaching out for healing.

During the delay caused by the woman's cure, Jairus's daughter died. According to Schüssler Fiorenza, bleeding was death for women because it signified isolation from community. The emergence of womanhood for Jairus's daughter had fatal consequences, but the previous healing event hints at a reality already present. Jesus declared the child was only asleep. His function was to awaken her. Her adult female status was not denied but was affirmed as positive and active.

The context of the text points beyond personal illness to the social nature of the women's ailments. Behind the two women stand countless others who are encouraged to claim their femaleness. They are images of the removal of death and return to life of all women in the *basileia*.

The defiling element of womanhood is healed, according to Schüssler Fiorenza's interpretation.

If we use Schüssler Fiorenza's contention that women represent, at least in some of the Gospel stories, the marginal in society, the stories of the hemorrhaging woman and Jairus's daughter take on heuristic theological implications. The woman's flow of blood, her suffering, is the mark of her isolation, the absence of the flow of connectedness that we must have to be whole. She represents the brokenness of our human connections and her courage restores the flow of connectedness. As metaphors of exclusion, the women represent those who have been excluded or denied full participation in the church on the basis of factors over which authorities and experts have no power. Gender, race, sexual orientation, age, culture, language, and all other aspects of life that are part of the complex nature of selves are denied as reasons for exclusion and subordination.

This social aspect of the story can only make sense if the women are specifically understood in their femaleness under patriarchy. Without the specificity of gender and context, the stories' metaphorical qualities are lost. As a metaphor for exclusion, the wounded are called to action. In faith in their own worth, the wounded are called, despite fear of the consequences, to search until a source of healing opens itself, to refuse despair, and to act for wholeness. Thus the children who will become the next generation are given life.

The interlocking of the women's stories also make them images of one person. In acknowledging her own vulnerability, the woman was returned to wholeness. As a woman, she had sought a source to remove her isolation and restore her to wholeness. In doing so, she created the possibility for the child in her to come back to life. As a child in the sleeping girl, she is helped by someone who loves her and brings healing to her, but her own courage makes that act possible. In joining the two stories, the two aspects of one woman are returned into the wholeness of woman/child. Vulnerability reveals God.

This presence of vulnerability is brought to an important revealing moment in the passion narrative. In dying, Jesus becomes vulnerable, the image of the destroyed child. Immediately before his death, the twelve who would eventually desert Jesus are shown as still expecting a triumphant messiah. But Jesus did not defeat Rome with the armies of God. Instead he died in the hands of Rome. The shock of defeat of messianic hopes seems to have been profound for those disciples who expected deliverance from an omnipotent God and a triumphant messiah. In identifying with those who symbolize such power, the fleeing disciples felt guilt and understood Jesus' death as deserved by everyone. They saw Jesus's death as a death for them, so that they might live.

However, some of the disciples understood how much they had misunderstood divine power and Jesus' mission. The harsh reality of his death shattered their expectations and cast his words and deeds in a different light. These disciples, women and men, made sure Jesus did not die abandoned and betrayed. They represented those who, through their participation in the Jesus movement, had experienced the liberating, empowering presence of love. The women at the resurrection also represented a caring, patient presence that could be wounded but not denied. Though frightened, they did not leave Jesus alone.

Divine presence as love, as connectedness, had come to the community through the wounded. Now, in the passion narrative, Jesus becomes the symbol of woundedness, such that the event of his death becomes a revelatory moment, pointing us toward vulnerability. In being bound with the vulnerable who accompany him to his death, Jesus is exposed as one among them, too wounded to suffer alone. In this alternative interpretation of the death and resurrection, gleaned from minor notes and undercurrents in the Gospel narratives, life surfaces through connection.

The centurion's confession at the end of Mark points to the incompleteness of the narrative. If Jesus' death was the end of the story, the illumination of divine presence is incomplete, for the relationships would be severed. They are not. The women return to his grave to claim him. When the stricken Jesus leaves them, they bring back his presence as a part of themselves, as a vision. The visionary-ecstatic images of the resurrection are expressed in various forms in the Gospels. In claiming life for themselves, the community transforms Jesus Christ into Christa/Community.

The resurrection of an abandoned Jesus is a meaningless event. The resurrection is given meaning by the witnesses who saw him die, marked his grave, and returned. These witnesses refused to let death and oppression defeat them; they remembered his presence to them; and they affirmed the divine presence among them. The persistent affirmation that oppressive powers would not have the last word, the refusal to give up on life, and the maintenance of healing presence give meaning to the resurrection as a profound affirmation of *this* life, of the lives of those who live here and now and who cry out for healing and deliverance. The final circle of wholeness is provided by those women who, in their response to the death of Jesus, refuse to abandon him, stealing finality from defeat and disconnection. They understand their own fragility, but they refuse to give up on themselves and those they love. To understand the meaning of Christ, we must be willing to acknowledge the Child in ourselves and in each other and we must acknowledge our interdependence. In those moments of acknowledgment the tomb of death becomes a womb of life.

CONCLUSION

In the patriarchal family we find structures and practices that produce male dominance and sharp gender differences. The family even in its modern forms continues to transmit an orientation of control toward children. Children are seen as extensions of adult needs. In patriarchal systems self-acceptance and intimacy are difficult achievements. We find instead a legacy of dominated and abused children. That legacy transmits itself theologically in Christian doctrines and images that reflect our need for a perfect, good, omnipotent parent. To break free of and be healed of patterns of abuse, we must find the metaphors that lead us back to the Child, the vulnerable center of ourselves that carries our demons and wounds and that is the center of our power to connect.

To be speaking of weakness, vulnerability, and interdependence in the late twentieth century may seem like folly. The militaristic structures of patriarchy seem determined to rush our planet into a final all-encompassing death. What possible power can fragility, grace, gentleness, and vulnerability have to stop the machines of patriachy? Because we have believed in a divine being capable of such destructive power, we have made ourselves in that image. To continue to rely on such power will not see us out of our morass. To trust in the fragile Child, to challenge the powers of destruction with love, interdependence, care, and compassion, we must be courageous. But it is absolutely necessary—and a little Child will lead us.

NOTES

1. Charlotte B. O'Kelly and Larry S. Carney, *Women and Men in Society: Cross-Cultural Perspectives on Gender Stratification*, 2d ed. (Belmont, Calif.:

Wadsworth Publishing Co., 1988), esp. 90–91. See also Gerda Lerner, *The Creation of Patriarchy* (New York: Oxford University Press, 1986), for a discussion of the complex factors that produce male dominance. Neither work asserts that all foraging societies are egalitarian, but that egalitarian societies occur more characteristically with foragers than in any other social organization.

2. See Alice Miller, *For Your Own Good: Hidden Cruelty in Childrearing and the Roots of Violence* and *Thou Shalt Not Be Aware: Society's Betrayal of the Child* (New York: Farrar, Straus & Giroux, 1984). Miller discusses the similarity between religious ideas of God and images of parents created by abused children. Lerner, *Creation of Patriarchy*, claims that benign paternalism develops out of patriarchal family relations and mitigates dominance by providing a sense of mutuality through the presence of reciprocal rights and obligations. "The dominated exchange submission for protection, unpaid labor for maintenance" (p. 239). For paternalism to function, the dominated must believe that their protectors are the only authorities capable of fulfilling their needs.

3. Carol Gilligan, *In a Different Voice: Psychological Theory and Women's Development* (Cambridge: Harvard University Press, 1982), raises the question of the value of a different perspective represented by some women that differs from men. See also the summary of Nancy Chodorow, *The Reproduction of Mothering: Psychoanalysis and the Sociology of Gender* (Berkeley and Los Angeles: University of California Press, 1978), in the following paragraph. Gilligan uses Chodorow's work in object-relations theory to support her thesis.

The issue of the role of biology in gender differences is not settled in feminist theory. While no feminist denies the importance of socialization in the production of gender difference, the extent to which gender identity is biologically grounded is still not clear. See Susan Basow, *Gender Stereotypes: Traditions and Alternatives* (Belmont, Calif.: Brooks/Cole, 1986), for a discussion of the research; and Hester Eisenstein, *Contemporary Feminist Thought* (Boston: G. K. Hall, 1983) for a discussion of the theoretical implications of grounding gender difference metaphysically rather than culturally. Lerner (*Creation of Patriarchy*) and O'Kelly and Carney (*Women and Men in Society*) also discuss the question of the relationship between biology and culture.

4. For an extensive discussion of the impact of gender difference on views of power, see David McClelland, *Power: The Inner Experience* (New York: Irvington Publishers, 1975). He describes the male view of power as both hierarchical and haunted by a tragic sense of the inevitability of failure.

5. I am not convinced that all gender difference is socially and historically constructed, but I believe extremely divergent forms of masculinity and femininity are not biologically grounded, based on evidence from crosscultural studies of gender difference. See Basow (*Gender Stereotypes*), Lerner (*Creation of Patriarchy*), and O'Kelly and Carney (*Women and Men in Society*). We can

free ourselves from rigid gender roles because even when biology is a factor in our lives, it interacts profoundly with environmental factors. Hence, to argue that biology might be a factor in gender-differentiated behavior does not mean such differences are rigidly fixed, or that differences along gender lines are greater than differences among members of one gender. Nor do biologically grounded differences mean such differences must be hierarchically valued.

6. For an extensive discussion of the separative self of androcentrism and the feminist view of life as connected, see Catherine Keller, *From a Broken Web: Separation, Sexism, and Self* (Boston: Beacon Press, 1986).

7. Miller, *For Your Own Good.*

8. This is not to say that all sexual differences are false, but that many socially constructed gender differences serve political purposes that support the power structures of patriarchy. These differences are part of a socialization process that denies individual persons access to essential parts of themselves.

9. Harriet Goldhor Lerner, *The Dance of Anger: A Woman's Guide to Changing the Pattern of Intimate Relationships* (New York: Harper & Row, 1985).

10. Miller, *For Your Own Good,* xi.

11. Mary Daly, *Beyond God the Father: Toward a Philosophy of Women's Liberation* (Boston: Beacon Press, 1973). See also Charles Hartshorne, *Omnipotence and Other Theological Mistakes* (Albany: State University of New York Press, 1984); and idem, *The Divine Relativity: A Social Conception of God* (New Haven: Yale University Press, 1967).

12. Quoted by Barbara Deming in *We Are All Part of One Another: A Barbara Deming Reader,* ed. Jane Meyerding (New Haven: New Society Publishers, 1984).

13. Alice Miller's work has led me to this conclusion, which I presented in a paper at the 1985 national meeting of the American Academy of Religion. The presence of religious ideas that support child abuse is most clearly articulated by Miller in a section on Job in *Thou Shalt Not Be Aware.*

14. Consciousness-raising was one of the trademarks of the wave of feminism that marks its beginning with Betty Friedan, *The Feminine Mystique* (New York: Dell Publishing Co., 1973).

15. Nelle Morton, "The Goddess as Metaphoric Image," in *The Journey Is Home* (Boston: Beacon Press, 1985), 147–75.

16. See Elisabeth Schüssler Fiorenza, *In Memory of Her: A Feminist Theological Reconstruction of Christian Origins* (New York: Crossroad, 1983).

17. Ibid.

4

Sexual Violence: Patriarchy's Offense and Defense

KAREN L. BLOOMQUIST

The primary cause of violence in this country is related to notions that connect masculinity and violence, plus the power imbalance between the sexes that allows men to act out this dangerous connection. For it to be considered unmanly to be powerful, dominant, or violent, great changes will have to be made.

—Diane E. H. Russell, *Rape in Marriage*

PATRIARCHY'S OFFENSE

Sexual violence is viciously intertwined with patriarchy. Violence against women can be seen as the outgrowth of patriarchal social constructs that define the relationship between women and men as one of subordination and domination. Patriarchy is the complex of ideologies and structures that sustains and perpetuates male control over females. This historically created gender hierarchy of males over females functions as if it were natural. Patriarchy becomes a moral system in which power or control over is the central value not only in male-female relationships but throughout the social and natural order.

It is this control-over mandate within patriarchy that makes it prone to violence. If one's identity is rooted in exercising control over another, one is tempted to go to any lengths to assure or reassert that control. As Jessica Benjamin notes,

Violence is a way of expressing or asserting control over an other, of establishing one's own autonomy and negating the other person's. It is a way of repudiating dependency while attempting to avoid the consequent feeling of aloneness. It makes the other an object but retains possession of her or him.[1]

Various expressions of popular culture assert that violence is the means by which men can stay in control or regain control over "their" women. It is an offensive tactic that serves the interests of patriarchy.

Sexual violence is both socially constructed and individually willed. Individuals *choose* to exercise violence, but that choice is influenced deeply by how one experiences one's place in the overall social order. Perpetrators of sexual violence come from all social strata and are influenced by a wide variety of factors, but the way in which the structure and ideology of patriarchy are intertwined with capitalism makes the possibility of violence insidious. The relationship between patriarchy and capitalism in men's lives is likely to play itself out in different ways, depending on their class position.[2]

Under the patriarchal system in the United States, a poor or working-class male for whom the choices in life have been severely limited due to the dynamics of capitalism is likely to feel real powerlessness in society. That feeling, combined with a popular culture in which violent imagery is often quite explicit, heightens the temptation to resort to violent control of women in order to assert manhood and gain at least some sense of personal power vis-à-vis other *men*. Control over a woman becomes the means of establishing identity as a man. In a working-class culture, this is the formula for male dignity and worth; it also helps account for much homophobia. Home becomes the place where a married man feels he can exercise his authority. As a young worker observed,

> Not only does the need for respect through power play itself out at home, but home becomes the very blame for that powerlessness in the first place, and so more and more of that anger and frustration experienced at work is brought crashing home on the innocent victim.[3]

On the other hand, the professional/managerial man is accustomed to exercising control over people in his public roles, sanctioned by a corporate culture that is competitive and *implicitly* violent. When his exercise of public power is frustrated, the temptation is to take it out on a woman (spouse, lover, or coworker) who has consistently lacked public power and is expected to be always nurturing of him. She becomes the scapegoat for the violence he cannot express in the public realm for fear of jeopardizing his power.

In each case, the individual's value as a man is shaped by the social relations of capitalism, which insists that one is what one makes of oneself and results in self-blame when one fails.

It's this "back-against-the-wall-so-put-'em-up-and-fight" option that is a real breeding ground for domestic violence. It is a struggle for survival, a struggle to breathe, a struggle to beat back the overwhelming oppression being inflicted by a fellow victim too wrapped up in his own "world of pain" to fully grasp his complete cooperation in the system he hates.[4]

To heal their wounded identity, men are accustomed to turn to women for affection, nurture, and healing. As the mother becomes the target of the young boy's anger when his needs are not met, so now a woman becomes the target for the adult man's pain, which is likely to be bottled up and to erupt in unexpected ways because of the patriarchal taboos against males talking about their pain and weakness. When this parasitic relationship between patriarchy and capitalism is compounded by the wounds inflicted by racism, the temptation to respond violently becomes even more complicated.

PATRIARCHY'S DEFENSE

This systemic nature of the plague of sexual violence is being brought increasingly to public attention. The need to challenge the patriarchal assumptions operating in society is becoming more apparent. And some change is beginning to occur. Women are increasingly visible in at least token positions in the public arena, although most continue to find their employment in low-paying, low-status jobs. Some women *are* speaking out, asserting their strength as part of a whole movement to counter the many expressions of sexual violence, supporting the victims, and effecting changes in public policy and personal relationships. Such developments are essential in challenging sexual violence as an acceptable offense of patriarchy.

However, as the presuppositions and operating tactics of patriarchy are questioned, challenged, and begin to lose their credibility, the violence does not necessarily go away but appears in new, often more subtle expressions as defensive tactics of patriarchy. An institution may claim to be opposed to sexism, but the sexual harassment experienced by the women who work there may worsen. As the civil rights movement and other social movements have demonstrated, it is easier to change public structures than private attitudes and behaviors. When women begin to gain some public power, what still endures, especially in one-on-one relationships, is the historically created gender hierarchy of men over women and the domination it legitimates. As long as that domination continues to hold sway, some men will continue to find an excuse to batter the females with whom they are in relationship. Furthermore, the forms that battering takes will probably continue to proliferate, as one form after another becomes more socially unacceptable.

The significant changes in the status of women that have occurred during the past two decades and that have been sending tremors through our social order are opposed publicly by a vocal yet small remnant who yearn to turn back the clock. They react vehemently and at times violently, especially to the loss of patriarchal control over women's pro-creative power. Such violent reactions are not surprising when we remember that the defining feature of patriarchy is control or power over women. That control over must be maintained *at any cost* because it is the core moral value that generates males' sense of identity and worth in this society. As one man put it, "Violence is a way to keep control, to maintain your identity."

My experience and observation is that institutions and men of a liberal persuasion now find themselves in a dilemma. It is increasingly unacceptable to sanction patriarchy publicly. Most proclaim their support for women's equal rights and accept the rationality of such appeals. But at some less than rational level there still is the gnawing sensation of having to exercise control over someone or something in order to have any sense of dignity or value.

The liberation of women is affirmed in the abstract, but many of the old assumptions continue to operate, often unconsciously, in men's interpersonal relationships with women. A professional woman may experience polite respect in public settings from the same man who in private lapses into sexually harassing behavior to remind her that she's still a woman. Many liberal men speak out against patriarchy in the public order, but in their more private relations with their spouses, female friends, or colleagues, they continue to exert subtle and not so subtle control over women. A woman continues to be valued or devalued according to her sexual attractiveness or how "good" a wife or mother she is.

The threat of the male prerogative being given up or taken away evokes in men panic and a feeling of impending chaos that may result in a violent reaction. Those women with whom such a man is in close relationship become the most likely targets of violence, be it physical, mental, or spiritual. Such violence is a response to what is sensed to be the destruction of previously absolute, actually unjust social structures. Whether the social order has really changed that much, whether many women actually do find themselves in positions with public power is not the issue. What is important is the public rhetoric that asserts that to be the case.

Thus, some white middle-class males who are accustomed to having social power are now expressing feelings of having been passed over for positions in favor of women. There is a mounting backlash in some churches that have committed themselves to inclusiveness. The frustrations of such men are in turn channeled into their private relationships with women. Working-class and poor men, as well as most men of color, have never had a sense of real social power. The scorn many of them have toward women coming into their own voice and power is more direct and usually not very subtle.

Patriarchy has provided the legitimation of sexual violence. As sexual violence is challenged, so too are its patriarchal underpinnings. But insofar as the latter have provided the chief anchor for male identity and sense of self-worth, a crisis erupts. The desire for *nomos* can no longer be satisfied by clinging to an unjust patriarchal system of values. Although it is a crisis that men must deal with, it cannot be ignored by those women who are married to men, are mothers of sons, or work in pervasively male institutions.

In those rare instances in which men no longer exercise control over the women with whom they are in a personal or work relationship, it is often at the sacrifice of real social power in the wider society. These are the men who, for example, follow their wives' careers at the sacrifice of their own, and may be publicly lauded but are privately viewed as less than men. They become threatening to those men who give verbal support to equal rights for women but who continue to base their own identity on patriarchal measures of value.

In the public arena things may be changing, but there is a real lag in dealing with the more private, emotional agenda. The increasing presence and participation of women in the public arena is one thing, but most men have barely begun to deal with the deep-rooted emotional agenda that such a shift evokes. The entry of women into positions of leadership in society and the church is only the beginning of the struggle. It points to the need for a deeper conversion, with spiritual/ religious dimensions.

CONVERSION FROM PATRIARCHY

Significant changes in male-female relationships have occurred, usually through dialogue initiated by women. But insofar as patriarchy is retreating to a defensive posture, we may be reaching a volatile point where dialogue is not likely to touch the emotional depths of many men as the structures of patriarchy begin to crumble. Patriarchal dictates are still sufficiently in place to remind men that it is not acceptable to be *too* vulnerable. In these critical times, men need to be in far deeper dialogue with one another before the possibility of more meaningful dialogue with women can emerge.

Until that occurs, we should not be surprised at the conflictive, often violence-laden dynamics that impact the relations of men and women, even in justice-minded religious institutions. When sexual harassment or violence erupts, it has commonly been viewed and treated as a woman's problem: It wouldn't have happened if she hadn't been present. Instead, serious attention must be given to the deep-rooted emotional, spiritual agenda confronting men as patriarchy becomes less credible. This is probably the biggest obstacle standing in the way of women's continuing struggle for justice.

A crucial theological agenda in the conversion from patriarchy is the transformation of God-language and imagery. Exclusively male imagery and language for God continues to legitimize patriarchy and the paradigm of male "control over" that undergirds the violence-laden situation we find ourselves in today. It is not that male God-language is in itself generative of violence, but that it comes to function that way within the central power-over dictates of patriarchy. To continue to use exclusively male references to God while we claim to be opposed to patriarchy is to reinforce the schizoid situation discussed earlier. The hostile reactions that female references to God continue to arouse in many church-related and secular audiences are indicative of the deep symbolic and emotional hold that patriarchy still has on most people. Rationally we *know* God is not male, but "He" still provides the security and order that many seek, thereby justifying the use of violence to maintain that order. Changing God-language and imagery is not an elitist exercise but a key step in the conversion from patriarchy.

Alternatives to the usual paradigm of power viewed as control over need to be discussed, experienced, and modeled in our institutions, theology, and ministry, and throughout our public and private lives. Rather than viewed as something one has to the exclusion or diminishment of another, power and authority are exercised in community in a way that empowers and authorizes others. Feminists have offered a variety of more mutually empowering paradigms of power. Carter Heyward, for example, raises up the image of Jesus' *dunamis*, a raw, spontaneous, unmediated power that breaks down established roles of control and possession and sets the stage for new, more reciprocal relationships.

Although serious questions need to be raised about how traditional theological understandings of grace, the cross, and sacrifice apply to the situation of women today, the applicability of these understandings to the present male experience needs to be accented. The Reformation understanding—that we receive our dignity or worth (are saved) not by what we do but by God's grace—goes against the grain of both patriarchy and capitalism. It is no secret that a gospel that emphasizes not being in control has not been very popular with men, at least when applied to the central patriarchal mandate in their lives. No wonder more women than men are found in most churches! It has been far more comfortable for male preachers to proclaim a gospel of self-sacrifice and giving up control to women and other subordinated groups. This "gospel" therefore serves to legitimize rather than transform the situation and conditions of these groups. Understandings such as a "theology of the cross" (that God is revealed through suffering and weakness rather than through glory) need to be applied far more directly and deeply to the heart of the current dilemma of *men* in this patriarchal society. Women who are victimized by patriarchy need to hear quite a different, far more empowering, message.

Although we cannot assume that Jesus totally transcended the patriarchal society of his day, he is depicted by the Gospel writers as having resisted assuming a certain kind of divine power or control over others. He called his disciples not "servants" who are under the control of a master, but "friends" (John 15:15). Immediately after Jesus' identity had been established through his baptism, the devil strove to draw him into distorted images of divine power (Matt. 4:1–11; Luke 4:1–13). But Jesus resisted the temptation to exercise hierarchical, controlling power over others. He refused to enter into a sadistic image of divine power that would imply that God wills us to suffer masochistically ("throw yourself down") in order to demonstrate "His" saving power. His identity was seemingly not dependent on exercising control over others.

Today, our first priority is to empower women to resist the blows of patriarchy. As that occurs, however, we should not be surprised at the insidious ways in which patriarchy will lash back. It has been around too long. Fighting back is the only option it knows. Becoming more aware of the ever-changing offensive and defensive tactics of patriarchy as it functions in this capitalist society is essential if we are to make deeper systemic changes to end sexual violence.

NOTES

1. Jessica Benjamin, "Master and Slave: The Fantasy of Erotic Domination," in *Powers of Desire: The Politics of Sexuality,* ed. Ann Snitow, Christine Stansell, and Sharon Thompson (New York: Monthly Review Press, 1983), 285.

2. See, e.g., Michael Lerner, *Surplus Powerlessness* (Oakland, Calif.: Institute for Labor and Mental Health, 1986); Lillian Breslow Rubin, *Worlds of Pain* (New York: Basic Books, 1976); and Richard Sennett and Jonathon Cobb, *The Hidden Injuries of Class* (New York: Vintage, 1972).

3. Mark Zima, "Blue-Collar Feminism: The System's Final Irony" (unpublished paper, Lutheran School of Theology, 1987), 5.

4. Ibid., 10.

5

Christian "Virtues" and Recovery from Child Sexual Abuse

SHEILA A. REDMOND

On a theoretical level, Christianity unanimously condemns sexual violence, rape, for example, as morally, ethically, and religiously unacceptable. But sexual violence does occur within specific Christian settings. Witness the explosive and controversial phenomenon of children being sexually abused by members of the Roman Catholic priesthood, a problem, as is child sexual abuse generally, that is finally "coming out of the closet" and making headlines in both Canada and the United States. In such cases of child sexual abuse, the negative aspects of certain religious symbols can have an overwhelming impact on the developing ego of Christian children and cause subsequent difficulty in their functioning as adults. However, this question does not appear to be addressed by either those in psychology of religion or in articles relating to child abuse in religious publications.[1] My concern here is with those victims of child sexual abuse who grow up within a Christian environment.

Anyone who was sexually abused as a child has a difficult time resolving the issue of the coercion that is inherent in the abusive situation. A woman or man raised in a Christian environment and sexually abused as a child may be particularly vulnerable to an incomplete resolution of that sexual abuse. It is seldom, if ever, asked whether religious factors themselves play a role in the creation of the illnesses from which these children later suffer. Is there something systemic to a particular religion, in this case, Christianity, that allows for a society with a substructure of sexual violence toward children, thus making survival after abuse a difficult proposition?

The role of Christian teachings in this area is in need of open discussion. The search for contributing Christian factors to child sexual abuse is involved and intricate. I attempt here to begin the search by looking at one aspect of the problem. What happens to the children who have grown up in a Christian environment and who have been sexually assaulted by a priest, father, relative, or family friend—people whom they have been raised to revere, respect, and obey? Do the images of Christianity hinder their recovery from this devastating abuse? To begin addressing some of these questions, the impact of sexual abuse on the child must be discussed. Then I will focus on five specific attitudes Christianity holds as a fundamental part of its heritage and the role these attitudes play in hampering a successful recovery from the assault.

THE EFFECTS OF CHILD
SEXUAL ABUSE

The premature introduction to sexual activity through nonconsensual relationships can have a long-lasting impact on the growth and development of the child in her or his maturation to adulthood.[2] Sexual relations between an adult and a child are inappropriate and developmentally destructive for many reasons. Inherent in nonexploitative sexual relationships is the idea of equality, consent, and mutuality.[3] This type of relationship is not possible for a child in relation to an adult.[4] The information and the desire to carry on an adult type of sexual relationship are lacking. In this kind of relationship, the adult demands that the child meet needs that should be met by the adult's peers, and expects adult responses and understanding from a child who is developmentally unequipped for such responses. The child is forced into pseudo-maturity by the assault. On the basis of experience alone, she or he is ill-equipped to assess the potential dangers of adult/child sexual relationships. The child may have a difficult time determining just what is wrong with this relationship, why she or he feels uncomfortable. A child needs warmth, affection, and love; and confusion is created by the perpetrator in this respect. "An adult can see that the daughter's need for a father's affection does not cancel his culpability for sexually abusing her. But the child cannot resolve the conflict. . . ."[5] Neither the detrimental consequences for her psychosocial and psychosexual development nor the censure that will be applied if she attempts to repeat the behavior with other adults would be within her realm of experience.[6]

Long-term consequences almost inevitably surface. Even if there appears to be little immediate negative impact, depression often results. Child sexual abuse is now being discovered as one of the initial traumatic causes behind such illnesses as multiple personality disorders and eating disorders such as anorexia and bulimia. It is included in the history of prostitutes and of the abusers themselves. These problems can surface immediately or, if the act is blocked from memory, the impact of the abuse may not be recogizable until the teen years or even later.[7] Victims of child sexual abuse often show the same lack of self-esteem and inability to be involved in trusting relationships as do the children of alcoholics and children from backgrounds of physical violence.[8] What makes the similarity so understandable is that in almost all cases of child sexual abuse, the perpetrator of the act is someone the child knows, trusts, and loves. There is a betrayal of trust caused by the perpetrator's total rejection of the child's integrity as a human being.

The problems resulting from untreated child sexual abuse are devastating. It is almost impossible for the female adult who was abused to ever fully trust males or even other females. A negative self-image and feelings of inadequacy are coupled with an exaggerated sense of personal responsibility. These make up part of the developmental structure of the victim's personality. Any attempt to come to terms with the past and to overcome the effects of the abuse is a long-term project for the victim. She must go about reorganizing the involved, complex psychological structures that have been created during the intervening years of survival.

Children who have been sexually abused are often described, on the one hand, as responsible for, enjoying, or willingly participating in their own abuse.[9] On the other hand, it is also suggested that they are completely unaffected by the adult/child sexual relationship and that it will be forgotten and have no long-lasting effects.[10] The rape of an adult is now viewed as an aspect of assault and battery and not as an act of uncontrollable sexual passion; its devastating impact on the ego of the victim is recognized. In that same way, the sexual abuse of children must be seen solely as a violent act—with or without physical abuse.[11] It is perpetrated by an adult upon one too young to consent and too defenseless and powerless to say no.[12] It creates women who remain passive and victimized; it creates men who sexually abuse children and who relate to women and children from within a framework of authoritarian abuse.[13]

RECOVERY AND THE ROLE OF CHRISTIAN "VIRTUES"

The process of recovery from child sexual abuse is hampered by the fact that many children do not tell anyone of the experience until long after the initial assault.[14] The difficulty many adults have in discussing the problem further militates against the child receiving adequate counseling after the assault has come into the open.

There are important stages in effective recovery from abuse. The child must be allowed to talk openly about the assault and her feelings, without restrictions as to what she is supposed to feel or how she is supposed to react. The child involved must be convinced that there is nothing she or he did to make this adult, who is almost always a male, behave the way he did.[15] (These two stages of recovery are hampered, however, by the Christian "virtues" which I will analyze in the following section.)

Children attempt to understand, and within their own limited experience find some explanation for, the world. If, as is often the case in sexual abuse, the child remains silent or is allowed to "forget," the explanations the child finds will be furnished by the empirical data of the child's environment. When that environment is Christian, the images, symbols, rules, and expectations embedded in its religious values will play a major role in determining the answers the child will integrate into her or his developing psyche and upon which she or he will base future actions. Children's experience is limited by their age and understanding of, for example, "God the Father" as a symbolic way of referring to the ineffable.[16] As with many other aspects of Christian symbols, the explanations of sophisticated theological thinking are barely understood by many adults, much less by children.

The question of the values of Christianity is crucial. Religious values such as suffering, martyrdom, the role of the female, the role of the child, attitudes toward sexuality and marriage are all prescribed and proscribed in certain ways within the Christian religious structure. Children learn five virtues: (1) the value of suffering; (2) the virtue of forgiveness; (3) the necessity of remaining sexually pure (especially for little girls); (4) the fact that they are in need of redemption; and, most important, (5) the value that is placed on their obedience to authority figures. I will now discuss these five points from the point of view of the Christian child who has been sexually assaulted by someone she or he knows.

Suffering as Desirable

The justification or honoring of suffering can have a negative impact on the victims of child sexual abuse. The value placed on suffering in the Christian context has at least three important aspects. First, since the Christian god is just and merciful, if one has suffered, one has sinned. Suffering is part of the punishment meted out to those who disobey. Second, suffering and repentance teach humility and are the way back to forgiveness from this Christian god. Third, martyrdom, which is an extreme form of suffering, holds a special place of honor within the Christian tradition.

The impact of a sexual attack on the child makes the victim look for the answers to the question of why she or he has been made to suffer. Children are capable of drawing logical conclusions from the data they have been given.[17] Christian children are told that their god is just, merciful, and caring. If they are good, then bad things won't happen to them. A Christian child is unlikely to question the true value of either of the above statements when a bad thing happens. The logical conclusion is drawn: "I am a bad child." The child may decide that she was disobedient, did not say her prayers, was disrespectful, or lied. She may have been too proud or wasn't nice enough to her siblings. She must be bad or evil, and she certainly does not deserve to be loved.[18]

Victims of sexual assault suffer from self-destruction of the ego. One suffers because one has done something bad and is being punished. If one becomes truly repentant and humble, gives over one's soul to the control of the deity, then everything will be all right. Implicitly, the assault is destroying the integrity of the self. What better way to empty the soul and become humble than by being sexually assaulted as a child? This attitude toward suffering can then be used as a reason for not admitting the damage caused by the molestation. One can be blessed by stoically suffering this type of assault.

The martyrdom of females has often occurred in the context of sexual violence. The emulation of eleven-year-old Maria Goretti is a good recent example. When Maria became a saint in 1950, the Pope spoke of her as a model for all Roman Catholic girls, the St. Agnes of the twentieth century.[19] The mythology surrounding Maria Goretti is fraught with the best examples (or worst, depending on one's perspective) of the emulation of suffering, forgiveness, and sexual purity. According to her authorized biographers, Maria suffered just like Jesus and the Virgin.[20] Not only did this girl become a saint but her suffering was known by God before it happened. In fact, God had destined it. Her assailant should be happy that he had occasioned the wonderful thing which would happen to her—her sainthood. Maria Goretti was murdered because she refused to be raped; through suffering as she did, one might achieve some holiness. While Christians may explicitly condemn the act that brought about Maria's sainthood, her martyrdom teaches that suffering and the acts that caused the suffering are signs that she had been blessed.[21] Thus sexual assault, particularly if the actual loss of virginity is avoided, can be a blessing in disguise.

Forgiveness

Reactions to the sexual assault include anger, hurt, betrayal, and guilt. It is clear from the therapies of women who have been sexually assaulted as children that a necessary component of resolving the trauma of the assault is articulation of rage, anger, and hatred at being used, at the powerlessness of their positions when they were children. This mitigates against any demand for too early an emphasis on forgiveness and understanding the perpetrator and his crime as anything but unjustified and unforgivable. Forgiveness for the perpetrator is not a requirement for resolution of the abuse, and lack of forgiveness does not entail the need for revenge.[22]

One of the basic tenets of Christian thinking is the concept of forgiveness. One has to forgive one's enemies, turn the other cheek, forgive seventy times seven or, as interpreted, always. One also must seek forgiveness for what one has done wrong. True repentance is the only way to forgiveness. Again, the case of Maria Goretti contains an example of the Christian response. Maria forgave her assailant immediately and was repeatedly asked, despite her enormous pain, whether she did so. For the child who has been abused, her feelings must be accepted as they are exhibited and allowed to run their natural course. For the adult who is trying to overcome the earlier abuse, the requirements of reality, that is, hatred and anger, may be hampered if she or he is a devout Christian.

How does one truly repent when one has done nothing wrong? One must find something to repent and be forgiven for.

Sexual Purity

Child sexual assault denies that there is any positive value to the child's sexuality. Eventually the child has to realize that the crime in question was not related to her sexuality but that the sexual relationship was the means through which the adult most easily made use of the child for his own benefit. The utter selfishness and coercive nature of the act must be finally understood by the child.

Traditionally, Christian doctrine deemphasizes the importance of the body and focuses on the sexual act itself and the female body as the bearer of the worst sin. For females raised in the Roman Catholic tradition, the focus on sex, via adoration of the Virgin Mary, begins early. Those who hear of Maria Goretti are told that she died rather than allow herself to be sullied by the sex act. To quote one of her biographers,

> Maria's martyrdom was not an impromptu affair, but something well prepared for. But Maria Goretti did something more still: rather than take part in one single act of sin—an act for which she could have got absolution in five minutes in her next confession—she let herself be literally hacked to death.[23]

She wasn't "spoiled goods," something that the doctors checked out at the hospital immediately so that they could reassure her mother that the worst had not happened to her. At least Maria had died a virgin, much to her mother's relief. If you were assaulted as a child and you did not fight off the attacker to the death, you must be guilty of some sin, some inherent weakness; it must be your fault.

As it is told in *Crusade: The Bible Retold for Catholic Children*, the story of the creation of Eve underscores another aspect of the problem.

> God put Adam into a deep sleep, and took out one of the man's ribs. *He made a girl from the rib, and brought her to Adam.* . . . Ever since Adam's time, when *a young man* grows up, he leaves his father and mother and takes a wife. *A girl* who becomes a wife leaves her father and her mother, and lives with her husband.[24]

There is an accompanying picture of a female child standing side by side with a full-grown, bearded man who appears to be about thirty.[25]

Eve, the woman with whom human women are to be identified, looks like a prepubescent female, without breasts, pubic hair, or anything that might identify her as a woman. This Eve was the cause of humanity's fall from grace, the bringer of lust into the world. And in this children's Bible, she looks no older than twelve. The message is simple. If I look like Eve, I too must bring about lust. I must have caused this man to do this to me.

The Need for Redemption

A Jules Feiffer cartoon aptly describes one facet of the child's world. A little child is talking:

> I used to believe I was a good girl. Until I lost my doll and found out it wasn't lost, my big sister stole it. And my mother told me she was taking me to the zoo only it wasn't the zoo it was school. And my father told me he was taking me to the circus, only it wasn't the circus, it was the dentist. So that's how I found out I wasn't good. Because if I was good why would all these good people want to punish me?[26]

Children assume that adults are "good" and right. Because they depend on adult good will, they can easily develop a sense of guilt and responsibility disproportionate to their actions, particularly if this sense of responsibility is environmentally reinforced. If a little girl who grows up thinking she is good can develop the idea that she is bad, what happens to a child who grows up knowing she or he is in need of redemption?

The need for redemption is at the heart of the Christian belief system or "symbolic world."[27] Martin Luther felt that it was better that a child should be murdered than live in the world with the assumption that it is a good and glorious place,[28] and have its soul destroyed.[29] In many forms of Christianity, children are baptized for the removal of some genetically implanted evil.[30] The focus on the need for redemption creates a sense of unworthiness and, eventually, guilt. For the child who is sexually abused, this abuse can truly prove that she or he is in need of redemption. It proves that the child is unworthy of being loved, of being happy. This halts movement toward resolution of the abuse, and the solution is found in the internalization of someone else's crime. As one woman put it, in recalling her own abuse, "He started abusing me when I was five years old. This was when I was beginning my religious training which taught me that women were vessels of sin. It was my sin of incest that made him [i.e., Jesus] hang on the cross."[31]

SHEILA A. REDMOND

Obedience to Authority
Figures: The Patriarchal
Family Ideal

Underlying the whole issue of recovery from child sexual abuse, and child abuse in general,[32] is the question of the attitude toward authority figures. Children must be taught that they have the right to say no, the right to question authority, and the right to disobey. The nature of the childhood of the human animal is such that the child is dependent on the good will of the adult—parent, teacher, relative, or stranger. She or he is dependent on the adult for nourishment, shelter, and, most important, love if she or he can be expected to attain the status of a healthy well-functioning adult. A child must learn to say no: not just no to a stranger, but no to a father, mother, uncle, teacher, priest, or minister. A necessary component for the successful resolution of sexual abuse and its aftermath is this kind of reorientation of attitudes toward authority figures.

Christianity constantly underscores the value of obedience to authority figures, especially parental or quasi-parental figures. The commandment "Thou shalt honor thy father and mother that thy days may be long on this earth" has been seen by Alice Miller as being at the root of Western violence and its attitude toward children.[33] Children are raised to respect their elders, obey their parents. Daddy and Mommy; Uncle Jimmy and grandpa; teacher, minister, and priest know best. The adult is always right.[34] Furthermore, children assume either (1) that what the trusted father or parental figure is asking is all right or even that what is asked is part of appropriate child/adult behavior or (2) that if she or he refuses, then the love of the adult will be lost.

The foundation for this attitude toward authority is found in the anthropomorphic conceptions of the Christian deity as male and the human relationship to this god.[35] Although the theological position of Christian monotheism argues that one cannot assign anthropomorphic characteristics to its god, attempts to "desex" or use multiple anthropomorphic terms for this god have met with strong resistance in much of Western Christianity.[36] The Christian child sees god as the heavenly father who can do no wrong. And this father god willingly sent his own child to be killed. The picture of Jesus drawn for us in the Gospel of John plays an enormous role in the minds of most Christians. This Gospel emphasizes Jesus' self-knowledge and his willingness to go to the cross to die, uncomplaining. John's Jesus teaches that one must accept willingly whatever the father does, for whatever the father does is right, justifiable, and must be obeyed. What made the crucifixion right and unquestionable is that the end (salvation of the human race because of its need for redemption[37]) justified the means (pedocide). The father is the exemplar on earth of the image of the father god in heaven. It is not difficult to see how it might follow, then, that hitting a child, locking a child in a closet, or depriving her or him of sensory needs can be justified "for their own good"—the salvation of the child's soul.[38] This kind of religious symbolism tolerates violence in family life and justifies, in particular, violence against children by fathers and other authority figures. If it can justify this kind of violence, it is not far removed to say that it can tolerate, even if it does not condone, child sexual abuse, particularly if some good results.[39]

The Christian parent is the ultimate authority figure next to god, "him"self. In Roman Catholicism, the priest virtually stands in for this god. Witness the angry statement from the father of a victim of priest assault in Louisiana: "He's only ten years old, he thought the priest was God."[40] If a child's priest, minister, or father abuses her or him, it is only natural for that abused child, who is raised in a Christian environment, to find the blame within her or himself. Within the framework of patriarchal Christianity, the child is almost powerless to reject the abuse, she cannot tell anyone just how evil she really is, and therefore is severely hampered in ever fully resolving the damage done by the assault through the rejection of the internalized guilt.

Christianity has such a vested interest in the maintenance of the patriarchal family ideal or benign dictatorship model on the personal and institutional level that often Christians, too, would rather blame children than force personal, parental responsibility onto the father or any other adult male. In a case of incest involving a church elder, other members of the Christian community spoke on the father's behalf in court and accused his daughters of seducing their father. The abysmal response of the Roman Catholic hierarchy to the assault of children by their priests also forces us to recognize that there is a serious problem not just in the secular society, but within the Christian ethos itself.

CONCLUSION

Many of the virtues of Christianity make it difficult, if not impossible, for the child who has suffered from the effects of sexual abuse to overcome the effects of this abuse successfully and lead a rewarding existence as an adult—particularly in the area of interpersonal relationships. Whether or not there is something systemic in the Christian "symbolic world" that facilitates this kind of sexual abuse of children is a question that needs further consideration and delineation. However, it is clear that Christian beliefs do not make it easy for children who have been sexually abused to deal with the abuse. It is possible that some of the values I have discussed may at times have a certain positive connotation. However, to those who suffer the victimization of child sexual assault these same values and symbols can have such a negative impact that it is difficult to ever fully resolve the conflicts that arise from acceptance of these beliefs.

The beliefs briefly described here are part of the doctrinal fund of Christianity. They reinforce personal guilt and responsibility continuously and by various means. This has the most disastrous consequences for a child victim of sexual assault. Many people were raised in a Christian environment and also were sexually abused as children. Many still carry this child and this child's adherence to Christian beliefs around with them. Therefore, they carry around the burden of unwarranted guilt. Without frank and open discussion of the negative aspects of Christian doctrine, there will be great difficulty in resolving the lingering feelings of responsibility for a crime that has been perpetrated upon them—not a crime of sexuality but a crime that has an impact on all of us, a crime of power, coercion, and abuse.[41]

NOTES

*A version of this paper was first delivered at the Annual Meeting of the American Academy of Religion in Atlanta, November 24, 1986. I would like to thank the Social Science and Humanities Research Council of Canada for their financial assistance which helped to fund my research in 1986–87.

1. There are exceptions to this point of view; however, they are not found within the mainstream of religious thought. See, e.g., D. Bakan, *Slaughter of the Innocents* (Toronto: CBC Learning Systems, 1971); Steele and Pollack, "A Psychiatric Study of Parents Who Abuse Infants and Small Children," in Helfer and Kempe, *The Battered Child*, 2d ed. (Chicago: University of Chicago Press, 1974 [1968]), 93. See K. Neufeld, "Child-Rearing, Religion, and Abusive Parents," *Religious Education* 74(1979): 234–44, who claims to refute the comments of Steele and Pollack above. However, Neufeld actually substantiates

their claim that the religious values of the abusers (which included, among others, Catholics, Mormons, and Lutherans) were of a particularly fundamentalist type. The work of the psychoanalyst Alice Miller (*For Your Own Good: Hidden Cruelty in Child-rearing and the Roots of Violence*, trans. Hildegarde and Hunter Hannum [New York: Farrar, Straus & Giroux, 1983/1985]) is a primary example of a devastating explanation of the impact that strict adherence to the all-powerful Fourth (or Fifth) Commandment in the Christian religious context has had on child-rearing practices in the Western world. Note also S. Forward and C. Buck, *Betrayal of Innocence: Incest and Its Devastation* (Toronto: Penguin Books Canada, 1984[1978]), 32; and C. Bagley, "Mental Health and the In-Family Sexual Abuse of Children and Adolescents," in B. Schlesinger, ed., *Sexual Abuse of Children in the 1980s* (Toronto: University of Toronto Press, 1986), 37–38. Bagley discusses the work of Mimi Silbert on street prostitutes in San Francisco. She found that the majority of them came from middle-class families with a formal religious atmosphere. His reference to M. Silbert and A. Piven ("Sexual Abuse as an Antecedent to Prostitution," *Child Abuse and Neglect* 5[1981]: 407–11) does not refer to this fact. However, it is likely that this information is contained in the larger Delancey Street Foundation report of which this article is a synopsis. There are often misguided attempts to mitigate the negative impact of religious teachings by those in the religious field. The response of the Canadian Council on Justice and Corrections to the Badgely report on child sexual abuse in Canada (*Brief to the Minister of Justice Regarding "Badgely Report on Sexual Offences Against Children,"* Ottawa, November, 1985) suffers from the same problem as E. Hastings, "Child Abuse: Viewing It as a National Problem and the Church as a Resource" (Ph.D. diss., Claremont School of Theology, 1975). The rights and problems of the aggressor become the focus of both (see n. 15 below) and ultimately more important than the injury done to the child, although this is clearly not the intent of either.

2. Perhaps the title "The Common Secret" is even more appropriate. Ruth Kempe and Henry Kempe, who coined this phrase for child sexual abuse, were pioneers in the field of the battered child syndrome. Their recent work on child sexual abuse has led them to believe that they underestimated the impact of sexual abuse on many of the children they had treated. They now feel that, in many cases, sexual abuse was the primary and often sole initiating cause for the behavioral problems of their child patients (Ruth S. Kempe and C. Henry Kempe, *The Common Secret: Sexual Abuse of Children and Adolescents* [New York: W. H. Freeman & Co., 1984], 3–7). See also R. Summit, "Beyond Belief: The Reluctant Discovery of Incest," in M. Kirkpatrick, ed., *Women's Sexual Experience: Explorations of the* Dark Continent (New York: Plenum Press, 1982), 127–50.

3. M. M. Fortune, *Sexual Violence: The Unmentionable Sin: An Ethical and Pastoral Perspective* (New York: Pilgrim Press, 1983), 42–98; see n. 4 below.

4. D. Finkelhor, *Child Sexual Abuse: New Theory and Research* (New York: Free Press, 1984), 14–22; idem, "What's Wrong with Sex Between Adults and Children?" *American Journal of Orthopsychiatry* 49(1979): 694–96. Bagley argues against Finkelhor's position with regard to consensuality from the point of view of a child-rights position ("Mental Health," 39). However, Bagley's position is considerably weakened when read in conjunction with John Holt's *Escape from Childhood: The Needs and Rights of Children* (New York: E. P. Dutton, 1974). Furthermore, the child-rights movement has been used by pedophiliac groups to support their positions of, e.g., "sex before eight or else it's too late." The reality is they simply want to justify the adult's right to sexually use and abuse children and to disguise their opinions under the guise of child rights advocacy. See Florence Rush, *The Best Kept Secret: Sexual Abuse of Children* (Toronto: McGraw-Hill, 1980), 183–92; and Louise Armstrong, "The Cradle of Sexual Politics: Incest," in Kirkpatrick, *Women's Sexual Experience*, 109–25. See Joseph Shepher (*Incest: A Biosocial View*, Studies in Anthropology [Toronto: Academic Press, 1983]). This work on incest from the anthropological perspective may have profound effects on the work on child sexual abuse. Following Edward Westermarck, and through insights from his own work on kibbutz children, Shepher concludes that there is an innate aversion to incest in human beings. The incest taboo is not a creation of culture à la Lévi-Strauss and others; but rather, the aversion to incest created the family. His argument goes a long way in supporting the view that incest itself is "unnatural" and therefore destructive to the development of the human being. It would now be culture (e.g., the development of patriarchy) which created and supports sexual relationships with children as opposed to the more common idea that the culturally created incest taboo stops people from doing "what comes naturally." See also n. 15 below.

5. L. Froula, "The Daughter's Seduction: Sexual Violence and Literary History," *Signs* 11(1986): 635.

6. R. Kempe and H. Kempe, *Common Secret*, 55–58. This case study is just one example of the problems involved in helping a child who has been trained to behave in a sexual manner.

7. Eating disorders such as bulimia and anorexia nervosa, which are primarily female disorders, often appear to be connected with child sexual abuse. See Miller (*For Your Own Good*, 131–32), who relates these disorders to child abuse. The child now has some form of control in an otherwise powerless situation. For an extreme case of multiple personality disorder and child sexual abuse see F. R. Schreiber, *Sibyl* (New York: Warner Books, 1973). I would argue that there is a lack of understanding of the religious dimension of the problem in the analysis as presented by Schreiber. See Silby, "Sexual Abuse."

8. C. Black, *It Will Never Happen to Me* (Denver: M.A.C. Printing and Publications Division, 1982); "Emotional Hangover: Growing up with an Alcoholic Parent," *McCall's*, October 1984, pp. 161–63.

9. L. I. Tamarack, "Fifty Myths and Facts About Incest," in Schlesinger, *Sexual Abuse*, 3–15. See also Rush, *Best Kept Secret*, 183–92.

10. Rush, *Best Kept Secret;* J. L. Herman, *Father-Daughter Incest* (Cambridge: Harvard University Press, 1981), 153, and nn.; 185–86.

11. This point is extremely important since often there is no overt physical damage done to the child. Actual penetration causes damage but it is often the case that the adult/child relationship involves alternate sexual activity such as oral-genital sex, particularly with the prepubescent child.

12. The equation of sex and violence, which has too often been inherent in any discussion of sexuality in the Christian sphere, is aptly described and discussed, and some solutions offered, in Fortune, *Sexual Violence*. See particularly chap. 2, "Confusing Sexual Activity and Sexual Violence," 14–41; and chap. 3, "Reframing Ethical Questions," 42–98.

13. A. N. Groth with H. J. Birnbaum, *Men Who Rape: The Psychology of the Offender* (New York and London: Plenum Press, 1985[1979]); A. N. Groth, "The Incest Offender," in S. M. Sgroi, *Handbook of Clinical Intervention in Child Sexual Abuse* (Toronto: D. C. Heath & Co., 1984[1982]), 215–39; Rush, *Best Kept Secret*, 13–15.

14. Hence Rush's euphemism, "best-kept secret." See D. Finkelhor, *Sexually Victimized Children* (New York: Free Press, 1979). One of the agonizing parts of research in this area is that it is obvious that the sexual destruction of children has been recognized in certain medical circles for at least a century; e.g., in France in the nineteenth century many cases were recorded and published. See A. Tardieu, *Etudes médico-légales sur les attentats des moeurs* (Paris: J. B. Baillière et fils, 1862), in which the drawings and autopsy discussions defy description. J. M. Masson (*The Assault on Truth: Freud's Suppression of the Seduction Theory* [New York: Farrar, Straus & Giroux, 1984], 14–54) discusses Tardieu's role in Freud's medical training. Doctors working in the area of the battered child syndrome also bring some of this earlier material to light. It is difficult to accept the fact that countless children have suffered for years because the time was not right. In 1932, Sandor Ferenczi, as had Freud earlier ("The Aetiology of Hysteria" [1896]), indicted men as the seducers of children ("Confusion of Tongues Between Adults and the Child," in Masson, *Assault*, App. C, pp. 283–95); his work was summarily dismissed (Masson, *Assault*, 145–92). As has Alice Miller today, Ferenczi seems to have given far more credence and weight to the reality of the sexual, physical, or emotional pain his patients had gone through in their childhoods than did Freud. See, e.g., Sandor Ferenczi, *Final Contributions to the Problems and Methods of Psychoanalysis*, ed. M. Balint (New York: Basic Books, 1955). At the time, the public would never have accepted the implications of the reality of child sexual abuse. The implications for Freudian theory are only now being questioned and are violently objected to by those who cannot let go of yet

another "God" and his gospel truth. Ultimately, they refuse to accept the massive effect that abusive acts have on children, their perception of reality, and, as a consequence, the world they will structure in the future. See Rush, *Best Kept Secret*, 80–104; Alice Miller, *For Your Own Good;* and idem, *Thou Shalt Not Be Aware: Society's Betrayal of the Child*, trans. Hildegarde and Hunter Hannum (New York: Farrar, Straus & Giroux, 1984[1981]).

15. This is a problem with incest cases, particularly when family therapy techniques that take the position that everyone is a victim are used. The daughter or son—the only one without responsibility—is lost in the family therapy. I would argue that this criticism holds in all forms of family therapy for families in which children have been abused. This type of therapy is advocated consistently in the religious context; e.g., Canadian Council on Justice and Corrections; and Hastings, "Child Abuse." For further criticism, see Herman, *Father-Daughter*, 152, 185–86; and Bagley, "Mental Health," 44–45, an apparent retraction of Bagley's earlier position on the use of integrated family therapy in incest cases and of his attitude concerning the harmful effects of incest in general. For a synopsis of his earlier "functional approach" in dealing with incest, see N. Gager and C. Schurr, *Sexual Assault: Confronting Rape in America* (New York: Grosset & Dunlap, 1976), 42–44.

16. D. Heller, *The Children's God* (Chicago: University of Chicago Press, 1986).

17. M. Lippman, A. M. Sharp, and F. S. Oscanyan, *Philosophy in the Classroom* (Philadelphia: Temple University Press, 1980), 12–30.

18. The Deuteronomist conception of history found in Deuteronomy to 2 Kings is the basic foundation for the Christian view of its relationship with its god and the world. The clearest delineation of the Deuteronomist's position is found in Bernhard W. Anderson, *Understanding the Old Testament* (Englewood Cliffs, N.J.: Prentice-Hall, 1975[1957]), 136–64, 348–62. The impact of the Deuteronomist's theological thinking should never be underestimated in any attempt to reshape the Christian tradition. Christianity as the new Chosen People considers itself to have inherited the relationship of the chosen people to the Yahwist god.

19. Maria Goretti was assaulted by a nineteen-year-old male relative who had already approached her several times before the final assault. She fought her rapist, was stabbed fourteen times, and died later in a hospital. She has been used most recently as a model for Catholic youth in a papal address by Pope John Paul II in 1980, "Address delivered to the young people of Catholic Action from Sengallia diocese on the modernness of Saint Maria Goretti's message," *OR(Eng)* 47(659), Nov. 24, 1980, pp. 8–9. Her shrine was rebuilt in 1979.

20. A manual on how to become a saint—die rather than be raped. The message is if you let yourself be raped, you must be a bad girl. See Maria

Cecilia Buehrle, *Saint Maria Goretti* (Milwaukee: Bruce Pub. Co., 1956[1950]). John Carr, *Saint Maria Goretti: Martyr for Purity* (Dublin: Clonmore & Reynolds, 1950[1948]). A. Ball, *Modern Saints: Their Lives and Faces* (Rockford, Ill.: Tan Books, 1983), 163–73. See J. Coulson, ed., *The Saints: A Concise Biographical Dictionary* (New York: Hawthorn Books, 1960), 323, for a concise explanation of why she was canonized; she had plenty of time to make a conscious decision between death and rape: "People like Mary Goretti . . . have an ever-present realization that lightly to surrender one's bodily integrity, even to the most compelling needs of the moment, upsets the whole rhythm of the universe." See also M. Warner, *Alone of All Her Sex* (London: Wiedenfeld & Nicolson, 1985[1976]), 71–72; Fortune, *Sexual Violence*, 23, 64–66.

21. J. A. Loftus, "Victims of Abuse as Candidates," *Review for Religious* (September–October 1986) discusses candidates for orders who were victims of child sexual abuse and points out that many people in the helping professions come from a background of family violence. Nowhere, however, does he address the problem that some of these people are actually attempting to redeem themselves for what was done to them. Given the intergenerational nature of most abusive structures, without a full resolution of the abuse perpetrated upon them, these helpers, however well-intentioned, may actually never be able to help others adequately. I would argue that if victims remain closely tied to their Christian religious values and seek to work out their past in a religious vocation, they will be more likely to perpetuate abusive situations than change them.

22. Often the perpetrator will not admit any responsibility for the act or will deny that the attack took place. This makes resolution doubly difficult but not insurmountable; see n. 13 above.

23. Carr, *Saint Maria*, 10.

24. Maryknoll Sisters, *Crusade: The Bible Retold for Catholic Children*, no. 2 (Chicago: John J. Crawley & Co., 1955), 46.

25. Ibid., no. 2, 47.

26. Jules Feiffer, 1977.

27. N. Perrin and D. Duling, *The New Testament: An Introduction: Proclamation and Parenesis, Myth and History*, 2d ed. (Toronto: Harcourt Brace Jovanovich, 1982[1974]), 57–58, is one of the most succinct delineations of this idea. If the world is not evil and there is no original sin, why is there need for a redeemer? See, e.g., two recent articles for teachers in the Canadian Roman Catholic school systems, by J. Forsyth, "Canadian Catechism: Redemptive Meaning of the Cross Is Lost in One-sided Approach to 'Friendly' Religion," *CT Reporter* 9/3(1983–84): 44–46; and idem, "Redemption and Rationality: Does Catechism Play Down Dark Side of Life Struggle?" *CT Reporter* 9/4(1983–84): 34.

28. Martin Luther, *What Luther Says: An Anthology*, comp. Ewald M. Plass

(Saint Louis: Concordia Pub. House, 1972) 1:410–11; also in ibid., 3:3244–46.

29. Ibid., 1:428.

30. In some forms of Protestantism, baptism is taken solely as a sign that the child will be brought up in the Christian community until such time as he or she will choose to become a Christian of her or his own free will. However, original sin and redemption go hand in hand and there is consistent theological justification for this type of thinking. See N. P. Williams, *The Ideas of the Fall and of Original Sin: A Historical and Critical Study* (London: Longmans, Green & Co., 1929[1927]).

31. Phil Donahue television show on incest, September 1986; speaker is Roxanne Yesu. See also Forward, *Betrayal*, 172.

32. The problem of child abuse (of which sexual abuse is just one part) revolves around the role of the child within the family and society. It is increasingly clear that the patriarchal family structure has allowed the systematic devaluation of women as human beings, and intervention into the sacred family sphere has been difficult even when the wife has been severely beaten; often the wife accepts the structure and thus, the responsibility for her situation. Letty Pogrebin (*Family Politics: Love and Power on an Intimate Frontier* [Toronto: McGraw-Hill, 1983]) has shown how destructive this patriarchal myth is to children in American society. She presents a devastating picture of a society that has no place for its children and devalues their existence from birth. See Herman (*Father-Daughter*, 49–63) for a discussion of patriarchal justification for child sexual abuse. Children's rights are strongly advocated by John Holt in *Escape from Childhood*. Although Holt's picture is distinctly utopian, this book is a primer on the problems of childhood and the need for child rights.

33. Miller, *For Your Own Good*.

34. Donahue television show on incest, September 1986. The pain of the mother of five daughters who had been sexually abused by their father was accentuated by the fact that she was a member of a fundamentalist Christian sect which held strong patriarchal family values. She had raised her daughters to do as their father said, to respect and obey him. Only her second youngest daughter broke the silence.

35. The patriarchal god of Christianity was considered male almost exclusively until the recent advent of the feminist movement. While the criticisms of feminist interpreters of the idea of the male god have had an impact, there is still a large body of Christians who reject the notion of god as anything but male, as exemplified in the maleness of Jesus his son. The need for the destruction of the male patriarchal god of Christianity is passionately argued by E. Reynaud in *Holy Virility: The Social Construction of Masculinity*, trans. Ros Schwartz (London: Pluto Press, 1983[1981]).

36. J. A. Phillips (*Eve: The History of an Idea* [San Francisco: Harper & Row, 1984]) has made one of the most succinct and sound analyses of the development of god as male and father, and the impact it has had on the consciousness of a people.

37. Fortune, *Sexual Violence*, 219.

38. S. Ozment, *When Fathers Ruled: Family Life in Reformation Europe* (Cambridge: Harvard University Press, 1983), 146–47. Ozment argues that the rise of the Protestant patriarchal unit was a positive development of the Reformation. He downplays the impact of the violent attitude toward children, which was justified religiously by the reformation movement: i.e., that it is better to err on the side of disciplining a child than not to discipline—even if it killed him. He feels that he is redressing a wrong committed by other writers on Protestant family life in the Reformation. The same kind of argument is made by J. W. Miller in "God as Father in the Bible and the Father Image in Several Contemporary Ancient Near Eastern Myths: A Comparison," *Studies in Religion* 14(1986): 347–54. In this paper, Yahweh as father has saved the family from the horrors of the Canaanite Tiamat, Baal, and Ashtarte myths. See n. 32 above and Miller, *For Your Own Good*, for criticisms of this approach.

39. Armstrong, in talking of the society as a whole, asks probably the most pertinent question of all: "What is the nature of the powerful need on the part of so many men to preserve the permission to exploit their children sexually?" ("The Cradle of Sexual Politics," 124). Pogrebin asks the same question from a different point of view; if we justify violence against children, it is only a small step to justifying sexual use of children (*Family Politics*, 106). See also Summit, "Beyond Belief."

40. "West Fifty Seventh Street," NBC, August 1986.

41. Although its accessibility is limited by its language, there is a book in Dutch devoted solely to the topic of Christianity and incest which I recommend highly. It includes ten interviews with women survivors of incest who were raised in Christian environments; Annie Imbens and Inneke Jonker, *Godsdienst en incest* (Amersfoort, Netherlands: De Horstink, in samenwerking met de Vereniging tegen Seksuele Kindermishandeling binnen het Gezin, 1985). (*Religion and Incest* [Amersfoort, Netherlands: De Horstink in cooperation with the Society against the Sexual Abuse of Children in the Family, 1985]). Although its findings support my work, I received it too late for use in the writing of this article. There are no fast and easy answers to solving the problems of child abuse and Christianity. Cooperation is needed between secular caregivers, pastoral counselors, and members of the Christian community. Secular caregivers often underestimate the importance of the religious trauma associated with the sexual abuse trauma. Pastoral counselors are often inadequately prepared for the depth of anger, rage, and guilt in the adult who is attempting to resolve child sexual abuse trauma. Two books which, while

not dealing with the specifics of child sexual abuse, may serve as a starting point for those who are counseling abuse victims and children of abuse in a Christian setting are Marie Fortune, *Sexual Violence;* and Andrew Lester, *Pastoral Care with Children in Crisis* (Philadelphia: Westminster Press, 1985). The best way for any Christian caregiver to provide help is to absorb the findings on the sexual abuse of children, its long-term impact, and the specifics of treatment with the victims. If children can be well counseled during periods of trauma, and can discuss the ongoing problems that arise during the different periods of development, much of the long-term damage of sexual abuse may be mitigated. However, there remain fundamental questions that arise from problems of child sexual abuse, child abuse in general, and our attitudes toward children. Questions about authority, patriarchy, and human responsibility for evil must be seen with open eyes by theologians and church members. God may survive the questioning and the answers, but whether biblical and historical Christianity can survive in its present form is a question the future will answer.

6

Theological Pornography: From Corporate to Communal Ethics*

MARY E. HUNT

Acquired Immune Deficiency Syndrome (AIDS) forces all Christians to rethink their sexual ethics. I do so as a Roman Catholic. The Roman Catholic Church has been quick to issue statements but slow to provide any real insights into norms that will help all of us live responsibly and compassionately. The problem is compounded by the fact that people with AIDS are rarely invited to be a part of any theo-ethical conversation on the matter. I will try here to spell out the problem, namely, the archaic and privatized way in which most Christian ethical reflection takes place, and to hint at its solution.

The heart of the contemporary ethical dilemmas faced by the Christian community lies in the corporate mind-set that underlies our ethical behavior. We mirror in our moral reflection the worst heterosexist, patriarchal aspects of the corporate world. Then we wonder why our ethics do not work.

Until that mind-set is disassembled and reconstructed according to principles of inclusivity and mutuality and with a preferential option for those who are most deeply affected by its content, we will not be able to claim that the twentieth century was a time when Christian ethics flourished.

The stand churches take for or against homosexual behavior is important. But the deeper questions at hand are, Who is the "church" to decide these things, and, How do we do ethics from a feminist liberation Christian perspective?

Poor people, people of color, and those who are oppressed by the

United States policies around the world teach us that there is little to lose and much to gain from going to the heart of the matter. A hierarchical, elite, white, mainly male structure excludes most of us. That is what most mainline churches, seminaries and denominational bureaucracies look like. Since most Christian ethics emerge from these places, no one should be shocked at the results.

These structures provide little ethical guidance in the face of the AIDS crisis. As Sister Theresa Kane commented regarding women and the Roman Catholic Church, we must not look to institutions for what they are constitutionally unable to provide. The task is to be church, to be a regularly convoked assembly of a "discipleship of equals." We need to reflect on ethics ourselves, to be agents who shape a new ethical methodology as well as content. This is what it means to engage in constructive theologizing, rather than in simply critical or reactive theologizing. This is what it means to turn the corporate mind-set around and to put ethical reflection in the hands of those who form community trying to live "in right relation."

My approach to transforming the corporate model into a communal one involves three fundamental moves. First, I characterize the contemporary ethical reflection from the Vatican (and related ecclesial institutions, though I do not consider it ecumenically polite to critique them) as nothing short of theological pornography. Second, I look at the roots of the problem, focusing on the corporate nature of our ethical reflection. And finally, I suggest that we shift from this corporate approach to a communal approach, using AIDS as the impetus for urgency.

THEOLOGICAL PORNOGRAPHY

The term "theological pornography" came to me when I was preparing remarks for a conference sponsored by Catholics for a Free Choice in December 1986. I alleged that in coping with abortion, the Roman Catholic bishops were lining their miters with a new kind of silk, namely, theological pornography. The phrase struck a chord in many who have experienced recent person-hating, inadequate pronouncements.

Theological pornography is not a common expression. These are not two words that we are used to pairing. Indeed, it is hard to imagine how the discipline usually defined as "faith seeking understanding" or reflection on "that than which nothing greater can be conceived" might have anything in common with pornography, with *Blue Boy, Hustler,* or worse.

I decided against a hard and fast definition of pornography, preferring to follow the lead of the late Supreme Court Justice Potter Stewart, who said that he could not define it. Rather, he stated, "I know it when I see it." I am deeply indebted to feminist theorists like Susan Griffin for their helpful analyses of pornography.[1]

I choose instead to approach pornography using three simple but inclusive categories. First, *pornography objectifies persons.* It makes them the object of perverted fantasies that bear little resemblance to real life. Second, *pornography trivializes sexuality.* It turns sexuality into distorted, usually violent images of women and children (sometimes men as well) subjected to the whims of others. Third, *pornography leads to violence.* There is debate as to whether pornography causes violence by suggestion or inhibits it by allowing people to act out in print and on film what they wish to do in person. My claim is simply that pornography and violence are deeply intertwined.

The Ratzinger Letter

Theological pornography is born of this analysis. My primary referent is the recent letter by Joseph Cardinal Ratzinger, "Letter to the Bishops of the Catholic Church on the Pastoral Care of Homosexual Persons," sometimes called the Halloween Letter since it was released in late October 1986.[2]

Among the letter's outrageous assertions is that homosexual tendency, and not simply homosexual behavior, is wrong. The letter states that the condition or tendency is "ordered toward an intrinsic moral evil and thus the inclination itself must be seen as an objective disorder." This view has not been warmly received by lesbian and gay Catholics. The letter, apart from its content, represents a corporate approach to ethics, which produces pornography so regularly that few readers give it much attention.

The letter is a classic in the genre of theological pornography. First, it objectifies persons, making no distinction between lesbian women and gay men. Neither does it make any distinction between persons who are homosexual by orientation, much less by choice, a category that does not seem to exist for the cardinal and his writers, and those who engage in homosexual activity but in fact may be heterosexual.

The letter gives no evidence of specific cases of homosexual behavior that modern psychology calls healthy, good, and natural. There is no effort to consult the data of the social or behavioral sciences. Careful ethicists find an abundance of psychological and sociological evidence showing that homosexuality is normal human behavior for a substantial percentage of the population.

Amazingly, there is little grappling with the basic theology of creation in the letter. Lesbian women and gay men are created in the image and likeness of the same God/ess as heterosexual people, not in the objectified, pornographic image of some lesser divinity.

Finally, the letter itself pronounces its message in the name of the whole church, as if this were the Word of God/ess. Such gross objectifications of persons, including the writer and team who produced this analysis, would be something to ignore if so many people were not affected by it. Like pornography available to children in the convenience store on the corner, this kind of dehumanizing and false portrayal parades as truth. It creates an environment in which sincere believers are seduced.

This letter does a grave injustice to people with AIDS anxious to make peace in their lives and to other faithful Catholics who strive to follow the church's teaching. Witness the quick falling in line of a dozen Catholic bishops in the United States who have forced Dignity chapters out of local Catholic churches. This is the sad result of objectification.

The Ratzinger letter is pornographic, second, because it trivializes sexuality. It takes an integral part of human beings—our potential to love and to be loved, to express that love in an embodied, genital way if we choose—and telescopes it into a narrowly focused fetish. Would that the writers had real experience of warm, loving, committed friendship in which sexual expression flows naturally. At the least they could have consulted people who do have such friendships before publishing such material in the name of the whole church. Instead, they imagine or project onto others forms of behavior that simply do not correspond with reality. They trivialize sexuality by condemning what is part of many people's responsible, human experience.

We are beginning to see high percentages of homosexuals in the allegedly celibate clergy. Some say that more than 60 percent of Roman Catholic priests are homosexual by orientation, though this is not a statement on sexual behavior. AIDS is beginning to take its toll among them. This gives us an idea, perhaps, of why the authors must trivialize what they do not understand. Such attitudes cause ecclesial genocide insofar as they encourage compulsive sex through compulsory celibacy. This is hardly the stuff of theological erotica which feminist theologians are attempting to develop.

The third characteristic of theological pornography found in the Ratzinger letter is the close connection between pornography and violence. The letter itself almost invites discrimination on the basis of sexual preference. It includes a disturbingly violent section: "When civil legislation is introduced to protect behavior to which no one has any conceivable right, neither the Church nor society at large should be surprised when other distorted notions and practices gain ground, and irrational and violent reactions increase . . ."

In the present homophobic, heterosexist climate, this sounds like an open invitation to violence. It seems to be a way of saying that boys will be boys. "Gay bashing" and instances of lesbians being attacked and raped for not conforming to heterosexist patriarchy are all but excused.

Perhaps the best thing that can be said for the Ratzinger letter is that it helped clarify what is really going on. We cannot forget that Rome used the same dynamic for the "natural resemblance" theory in 1976, which effectively erased the possibility of women's ordination. Women do not bear a natural resemblance to Jesus in the Eucharist.[3]

Again, we see the objectification of women and of Jesus, the trivialization of sexuality as if it were pertinent to ministry, and the unleashing of violence against faithful people who will be deprived of the eucharist due to a shortage of priests.

Reproductive Technology

Most recently, the same pornography appeared in a letter on reproductive technology.[4] As one might expect, the author was again Cardinal Ratzinger, and the dynamic is identical. In this letter, all forms of human reproduction are condemned except the most traditionally understood conjugal act within the confines of a (heterosexual) marriage and without any form of birth control.

The letter objectifies all who want to have children by other than strictly conventional means, whether a married or unmarried heterosexual couple, gay males who use surrogate mothers, or lesbian couples who use artificial insemination by donors. All are collapsed into a category of persons who would undo the order of creation while fulfilling their longing and right to have children.

It trivializes sexuality by making it into a one-dimensional activity always ordered toward procreation. The writers come up with an absurd exception, namely, artificial insemination in the context of conjugal activity, a contradiction in terms that left ethicists and journalists puzzled. The technical term is "gamete intrafallopian transfer." The exception is intercourse performed in a doctor's office using a condom with holes in it in order to fulfill the letter of the law. Then, the doctor would inseminate the woman without breaking the church law against contraception. While this is comical on the face of it, it is pornographic as well. That the institutional church would come up with the notion of a condom with holes in it, at a time when smart and safe sex requires condoms of the most effective sort, is, in my judgment, a legalistic trivialization.

Violence is encouraged in this Ratzinger product when people are abused in their spiritual homes. Many people will internalize presbiterogenic, or priest-caused, guilt over their efforts to have a family. Ironically, this happens in a church that urges people to procreate, but condemns them when they do it in a way that makes use of the best of modern technology. Like physical violence at home, this violence done to people in their spiritual home, the church, is of serious consequence.

Confining Christologies

Theological pornography is not the cottage industry of only the Roman Catholic church. Another example, *The Christa*, will prove the ecumenical nature of theological pornography. Edwina Sandys created a nude woman hung on a cross. It drew incredible commentaries in the secular and religious press. Outrage and horror were widespread at what some considered a sacrilege. Rosemary Radford Ruether summed up the problem brilliantly. "When people see a male crucified and hung on a cross they think of the ultimate symbol of tragedy. But when that same symbol is of a female, killed and hung on a cross, they see it as the ultimate symbol of pornography."[5]

Reading commentaries on *The Christa*, and even reading the reaction of those who consider the *Inclusive Language Lectionary* to be the castration of the Bible, I recognize the same peepshow mentality that I detect in Roman Catholic sexual ethics. Many people in seminaries and theological think tanks have such tiny, narrow views of Christianity.

Their Christologies are confined to minuscule images which they view for a quarter a peek. They see a little bit and think that it is the whole. They miss the point that theology is communal reflection, that theological erotica is the pleasure of deeply held communal beliefs. Such beliefs are not developed by peering into a window on reality but by engaging in the *praxis* of human liberation. They pass over the fact that Jesus is not real and available for private ecstasy paid for in small change. Rather, the fullness of the Christian message is in active response to the ongoing revelation of women and children whose bodies have been broken by rape, incest, child abuse, and domestic violence. All of these point to a world in need of more than movies.

The tragedy of theological pornography is that it usurps the energy that ought to be erotic, life giving, pleasure producing, and community building. Audre Lorde, in her classic essay "The Erotic as Power," observes that "the erotic offers a well of replenishing and provocative force to the woman who does not fear its revelation, nor succumb to the belief that sensation is enough."[6]

I suggest that the heart of the problem is not content alone, not simply theological pornography, but methodology. The very way in which we engage in theo-ethical reflection allows the pornography to exist in the first place.

THE CORPORATE MODEL FOR CHRISTIAN ETHICS

Theological pornography, like its secular counterpart, is the product of a system, a business that is geared to its content. This is the corporate model, which I consider inappropriate and inadequate for Christian ethics.

The women's movement has made great strides in the eradication of secular pornography. Women began not with the content but with the business aspects of pornography. An unlikely coalition of women on both the right and the left has attacked the corrupt business.

Feminists claim that pornography is not simply the individual choice and proclivity of a few who, under the First Amendment, ought to be able to look at what they like. Rather, feminists have discovered that porn is an $8-million-dollar business. *Playboy* and *Penthouse* have a combined readership of over 24 million, more than *Time* and *Newsweek*. In 1983 it was estimated that over 2 million U.S. households subscribe to cable television featuring pornography. Hence, pornography is not a few people's perverse hobby, but a national and international business.

It is somewhat more difficult to come up with parallel statistics for theological pornography. But it is part of a huge corporate network, which receives and disseminates this material in every nation, diocese, and parish in the world through national bishops' conferences. Theological pornography receives air and print play in the secular media. It is another business that shapes culture while being protected by both the constitutional guarantee of the free exercise of religion and the mantle of respectability of a major religion.

One approach to the problem is to claim fraud, to name the theological scams for what they are. For example, the same industry that allows women to pay tuition in seminaries knows full well that all Catholic seminaries are linked to a system that will not ordain those women. Likewise, another arm of the "business," liberal Protestant seminaries, is happy to take the tuition of gay and lesbian students without necessarily being a part of internal movements to permit ordination and placement of such candidates. This is the stuff of fraud. Admitting black, Asian, and Hispanic colleagues into the ministry of this corporate giant without parallel efforts to undo racism so that their ministries will be accepted is like television evangelists who take people's money. Good will is exploited and people are hurt.

But the equivalent of a theological Better Business Bureau will not be enough. The corporate model is simply antithetical to the effort to develop ethics in a community of believers. Four aspects of corporate life make this clear. These elements of our current ethical reflection need to be dismantled if we are to develop a theo-ethical framework adequate to deal with the current crisis provoked by AIDS, indeed, to deal with the many ethical issues faced by faithful Christians.

Ownership. First, the corporate mind-set focuses on ownership. Ownership in ethics is in the hands of a few. It is based on a scarcity model. Most owners are academically trained theologians and ethicists who work in seminaries and divinity schools. Those who work in "the field" have little input to the academic discussion.

In corporations, preferred stock is passed through high-level management. So too is theological stock "sold" to those who belong to the clergy, those who go to the right seminaries, those who imitate their professors. It is their duty to keep the corporation alive, to make decisions that reflect its best interests. The laity get the common stock, if any at all. But the owners pass on the wisdom and the chance to make decisions to their clones, the guardians of orthodoxy.

Secrecy, closed meetings, esoteric language among the owners guarantee that new agents, those who look different or speak different languages, will never be empowered. The best we can hope for is that at Christmas time there may be a bonus for the janitors who keep the corporation clean. We cannot hope that the fundamental structure of power will shift without a major overhaul. The issue is not so much content but methodology—in this case, power arrangement—which will guarantee orthodoxy.

Hierarchy. Another aspect of corporate life that has been passed on to the theo-ethical guild is hierarchical arrangement. Clear distinctions exist between those who pronounce and those who receive the pronouncements. Many are wary of takeover bids, people who might come along and make sense of ethical analysis in a new way, or even convince some people that the mores of our Christian culture need shifting. Moving up in a hierarchy takes people away from places where others suffer or grapple with issues confronting them. Alienation, rather than involvement, becomes a mark of Christian ethics.

Monopoly. A third mark of a corporate mind-set which has been taken over in ethics is the *urge toward monopoly*. We see airlines outbidding one another for control in the corporate world. The basic theory is to buy up the competition, gain a monopoly, and then raise prices as consumers stand by helplessly. In the theo-ethical world the urge toward monopoly is expressed by religious groups who claim to have a corner on truth.

These groups bar other manifestations of truth that might threaten theirs. For example, the National Council of Churches, in its effort to bar the Metropolitan Community Church from membership, clearly does not want to admit that lesbian/gay people might in fact be religious in the same way as heterosexual people. In the Catholic church there is a certain "buying up" of Episcopal priests who oppose the ordination of women in their own denomination. This shores up the Catholic prohibition against female clergy. Another case is the claim in some reputable graduate schools in recent years that Spanish is not a theological language. This preserves the hegemony of Western European and North American theology. All of these monopolies preserve the status quo.

The most insidious form of this dynamic is subtle cooptation. More than I have ever feared heresy, I fear being coopted, assimilated by a huge religious monolith that will blunt the edges of anything different, take into itself the best of the idea, and in so doing coopt efforts at change. If, for example, the Roman Catholic bishops ever decide to ordain women, the same bishops who currently oppose women's ordination will decide which women will be chosen and by what criteria. It is not the issue of women's ordination but the fact that the method or power equation does not change that is so alarming.

Networks. A final mark of a corporation, which is also present in the theo-ethical corporation, is the old-boy, old-girl network. Old-school ties, the right clubs, and the right sports all have their theological expression. The use of friends and contacts to assure that the right people will rise in the system—sending the best and the brightest off to study in Rome so that they will return with loyalty to the institutional church—is an obvious case in point. These networks, usually white, affluent, and well educated, assure that ethical reflection will not stray too far from the traditional mark.

Can the Corporate Model Be Changed?

I recently visited a theological think tank in Washington that shares its offices with a *contra* group. It was a shocking reminder of the theological corporation. But then I realized that I had seen the same ambience before in pictures of the Vatican Embassy (across from the Vice President's home in Washington), and also in person in some theological schools and church headquarters. I had heard the language, too. It sounded more like *Forbes* and *Business Week* than the gospel. I heard talk about the theological bottom line, the cash value of God-language, quotas, and preferential hiring patterns. Coffee was served properly on a tray by a woman, usually black or Hispanic. It made me sick.

But it also made me realize that theological pornography comes from such places. In a corporate atmosphere the pornographic product does not seem unusual. In an environment where money keeps the whole thing going—donations come from those who believe—we hardly notice theological porn. Those of us who talk about it are made to feel like temperance workers, as if the imagery were overblown, and as if we are really prudes after all.

Fortunately, the secular women's movement was not scared off by such possibilities. We take our cues from them as we dismantle this machine and elaborate the beginning of a theological erotica.

What new model will replace this corporate mind-set and eradicate theological pornography? The best example arises from the women who have worked to overcome domestic violence. Their content is important, but their method is instructive for our issue. They took the problem of domestic violence and began to solve it by providing shelters for women and children. Then they examined the legal issues, pushing for enforcement of existing laws and the development of new ones. Finally, and only after they had done a great deal of work in direct services, they formulated the theoretical framework in which to make sense of their experiences. Most of all, they involved the women themselves, the survivors, at every step along the way.

Note how different this is from the prevailing theo-ethical model. We usually begin with philosophical abstractions, then discern their theological ramifications. We conjecture about the ethics involved. If there is any time left over, we do something about it, calling it practical theology.

This is the corporate model. No one is promoted or receives tenure for doing something about a problem. Rewards go to those who stay at some remove from the problem in order to "think objectively" about it. We quote each other profusely when we write about it, anxious to shore up our distant wisdom with someone else's. It has taken liberation theologians to show us that the point of theology is God/ess, not quoting other theologians. And it has taken feminist and Marxist ethicists to show us that the point of ethics is to do something, not talk about it.

MODELS FOR THEOLOGICAL EROTICA

AIDS is spreading. It is causing death and anxiety at such a pace that ethical development is needed urgently. People deserve the best resources of their religious traditions at times when new issues force us to evaluate our behavior afresh.

The Roman Catholic church thus far has produced little more than the pornography I have discussed. The situation simply demands our best. A shortcut would be to ask the same people in the same institutions to provide us with ethical reflection on AIDS. But the better investment in time and energy is to use AIDS as an issue whereby dismantling the current ethical apparatus will lead to a new, inclusive methodology.

Let me suggest what such a renewed ethical enterprise might look like. A few caveats are necessary before proceeding. First, AIDS is a disease for the whole community, not simply something that "belongs" to gay men. Second, ethical thinking on this disease does not have a specially designed population. Medical experts assure us that by the turn of the century AIDS will be an equal-opportunity killer. Third, by choosing AIDS for my ethical focus I do not mean in any way to deny or denigrate the importance of other ethical issues such as domestic violence or the growing impoverishment of women and children. Rather, I choose a case that is closely connected to what the corporation has already considered, albeit inadequately, in order to sketch how the whole thing might look different.

I am trying to construct a cooperative model, one in which sharing and teamwork are the hallmarks. Such a model begins with the dismantling of the old to make room for the new. Hence I suggest alternatives to each of the four elements of the corporate model. Then I offer some reflections on the renewed product, which I call theological erotica.

Agency. First, ownership must be redefined as agency. Agency is the right and responsibility of those most deeply affected to bring their own views, experiences, and even shortcomings to the table. It is a community of ethical agents that will begin to formulate a meaningful, erotic theology. People with AIDS need to be an explicit part of the enterprise. Then we can talk about safe, smart sex for pleasure and for the deepening of relationship without leaving anyone out of the conversation.

Inclusivity. Secondly, the hierarchy of persons and values that so indelibly marks the corporation must be replaced by inclusivity and particularity on their own terms. I realize that this sounds like a recipe for chaos, but I would argue that until difference and the difference it makes can be articulated, we must resign ourselves to pornography. We will tend to objectify what we do not know, trivialize what we cannot imagine, and do violence out of fear.

Participatory models can work. In Bertioga, Brazil, for example, at a major feminist meeting, the question asked was not, Are you a feminist? but, What kind of feminist are you? This permitted many women to include themselves. I have used such a method with students. Instead of laying out strict definitions of terms, I ask people to look at their own experiences of a term, feminism, for instance, then look at the mainstream history of the concept and imagine how someone quite different from themselves might define it. Only then can we come to a commonly accepted working definition, clear that we are all agents in the development of the concept. This helps to change the power dynamics of those who have the right answer. It involves people so that they can internalize the ideas on their own terms. It is simply good strategy for community accountability.

Diversity. Third, the drive toward monopoly needs to be replaced by a concerted effort to accept diversity on its own terms, even when it is unpleasant. For example, lesbians have had to accept the fact that there are other lesbians who batter women, and we have had to devise a strategy for overcoming this violence. We have had to discuss various forms of sexual behavior, such as sadomasochism, which many of us find repugnant. We have had to listen to women's experience that is different from our own. We have found that we can live without agreeing. Truth comes on a model of plenty, not on a model of scarcity.

We are discovering that there is no one politically correct way to relate. Rather, we recognize the value of hearing and accepting various sexual expressions on their own terms. We do not need to judge gay men by calling their activities depraved. Nor do we want gay men calling us prudish. Only after we know a lot about each other do we dare to evaluate. For now, we need everyone in the community to pull together, since AIDS will not await our musings.

Religious Models. Finally, the old-boy, old-girl networks beg some better religious models. Perhaps Jesse Jackson's Rainbow Coalition or the notion of the *pueblo de dios* of our compañeros in Latin America would be helpful. At least we can say that a changing *sensus fidelium* suggests that ethical reflection is too important to be left to ethicists. Doctors, lawyers, researchers, health-care workers, people with AIDS, their families, and friends all need a hand in developing the ethical reflection.

As AIDS continues unabated, we are discovering that the politics of health care is essentially a corporate question with a corporate answer.

We are also learning something about the divine; we cannot control our own lives and deaths.

Diseases for which there is no cure take on the collective negativity of the culture. The society projects that negativity onto the most vulnerable. Susan Sontag, in *Illness as Metaphor*, made this clear in her discussion about tuberculosis and cancer.[7] I suspect that it is true of AIDS as well. But it is precisely in this cultural context that the resources of the Christian tradition, wrenched from their corporate context, become crucial.

Persons with AIDS deserve more than another battering in their spiritual homes. They deserve to identify the battering for what it is when documents such as the Ratzinger letter are issued. They do not need to tolerate the honeymoon period, as domestic violence theorists call it, when promises of better behavior issue from those who have acted violently. Nor must they tolerate the gradual buildup of tension that inevitably follows the honeymoon period in domestic abuse. They deserve nurture and support in their spiritual homes.

Persons with AIDS deserve to be a part of an ethical community that gathers the broadest and deepest knowledge that it can muster to face the complexities of a disease that knows no sexual preference. Virtually every traditional ethical issue—the right to privacy, the right to public access, the right to work and to medical care, the need for honest and direct dealings with one another, choices around childbearing—all need to be rethought in the light of AIDS.

None of this complexity is reflected in current theological pornography. The corporation has not yet had to face the reality that this disease will sneak through the careful screening of its members-only club. It will show up in the boardroom before we are through. Must we wait until it strikes to admit that a community of faith, and not a committee on rules, is needed?

It is in a community of faith that a theological erotica can develop. Persons, rather than being objectified, will be accepted as persons, subjects on their own terms. Fierce tenderness will characterize friendships between them.[8]

Sexuality, rather than being trivialized or blown out of proportion in the pornographic model, will be integrated into normal daily care for one another. Sexuality will be defined in a broad way to include a loving touch, a well-served dinner, shared silence, as well as enjoyable genital activity. But it will be integrated into relationships where work and love, children and pets, illness and vacations are part of the mix. This is how most of us live our sexuality in healthy, mature, committed relationships both heterosexual and homosexual. Why not let our experiences be the norm?

Finally, the violence that characterizes theological pornography would give way, in theological erotica, to the daily practice of nonviolence. Passion, excitement, physical ecstasy, comfort, and companionship are all part of the erotic life well lived. This is the stuff of grace; it is what bonds us with the divine and with one another. It girds us for the struggles for justice which will bring grace in ever greater abundance.

My hope is that getting to the heart of the matter, converting the corporate model into a communal one, will be a step toward building a community of faith able to support and nurture its people in crisis. This is the legacy of lesbian and gay Catholics to the church, whether it wishes to receive it or not.

NOTES

*This essay is adapted from a lecture delivered at Union Theological Seminary, New York, sponsored by the Consultation on Homosexuality, Roman Catholic Theology and Social Justice, and from the Women of the Decade Lecture sponsored by the Center for Women and Religion at the Graduate Theological Union, Berkeley, California.

1. Susan Griffin, *Pornography and Silence* (New York: Harper & Row, 1981).

2. "Letter to the Bishops of the Catholic Church on the Pastoral Care of Homosexual Persons," published by the Congregation for the Doctrine of the Faith (October 1986), under the signature of Joseph Cardinal Ratzinger.

3. "Declaration on the Question of the Admission of Women to the Ministerial Priesthood," published by the Sacred Congregation for the Doctrine of the Faith (October 1976), under the signature of Jerome Hamer, O.P., Titular Archbishop of Lorium.

4. "Instruction on Respect for Human Life in Its Origin and on the Dignity of Procreation: Replies to Certain Questions of the Day," published by the Congregation for the Doctrine of the Faith (February 1987), under the signature of Joseph Cardinal Ratzinger.

5. Rosemary Radford Ruether made this observation at a panel discussion on Christology at the American Academy of Religion, Atlanta, Georgia, November, 1986.

6. Audre Lorde, "Uses of the Erotic: The Erotic as Power," in *Sister*

Outsider: Essays and Speeches (Trumansburg, New York: Crossing Press, 1984), 54.

7. Susan Sontag, *Illness as Metaphor* (New York: Farrar, Straus & Giroux, 1978).

8. Cf. my *Fierce Tenderness: Toward a Feminist Theology of Friendships* (San Francisco: Harper & Row, 1987).

Dominion to Rule: The Roots and Consequences of a Theology of Ownership

CAROLE R. BOHN

Then the Lord God said, "It is not good that the man should be alone; I will make him a helper fit for him." . . . So the Lord God caused a deep sleep to fall upon the man, and while he slept took one of his ribs and closed up its place with flesh; and the rib which the Lord God had taken from the man he made into a woman and brought her to the man. (Gen. 2:18–22)

To the woman he said, "I will greatly multiply your pain in childbearing; in pain you shall bring forth children, yet your desire shall be for your husband, and he shall rule over you." (Gen. 3:16)

Man's authority to rule over woman is traced to God's intention in this account from Genesis 2 and 3. While many other biblical passages could be quoted to offset this view in favor of the equality of women and men in the eyes of God, the message that has pervaded the tradition is that women and their offspring are the property of men and hence subject to man's power. Throughout history, laws of various societies have attempted to limit the extent and means of man's control, but the underlying message, built into the words and structures of religious tradition, remains constant. By God's design, women and children are subject to men.

Religious traditions are relied upon to provide the underpinning of social norms. Yet it seems that social norms often give rise to religious traditions to justify them. Such is the "chicken-and-egg" nature of the origins of a theology of ownership. Most biblical exegetes consider the

105

Genesis creation accounts etiological stories; in other words, one might postulate that the attribution of man's ownership of woman to God's intent was a way of explaining, justifying, and preserving what was already an accepted social behavior. Therefore, the use of violence against women to maintain control is simply an extension of the rights of ownership.

This theology of ownership is pervasive and foundational to much of Christian thought and practice, though it is rarely named directly and most of its practitioners are unaware of it. It is manifest in the attitudes and behaviors of many clergy as well as in the very structures of most churches.

MANIFESTATIONS OF A THEOLOGY
OF OWNERSHIP IN THE LEADERSHIP
AND STRUCTURES OF CHRISTIANITY

In 1986, the Florida legislature overturned a law requiring anyone with knowledge of child abuse to report it to the authorities. The most vocal opponents of the law were a group of clergy—Protestant, Catholic, and Jewish—who argued that the relationship between minister and congregant is sacred and should not be bound by secular law.

Initially, these clergy came together in support of a Nazarene minister charged with failing to report a case of child sexual abuse. The complainant against the minister was the mother of a sexually abused six-year-old. Herself a member of the Church of Nazarene, the child's mother sought the advice of her minister when she learned of the abuse. She went to the minister, she said, because she wanted to be a good Christian woman and because she believed that he would tell her the "Christian thing to do." He advised her not to report the abuse to anyone else and said that he would take care of the problem. Later, the woman learned that the abuser, the child's uncle, was himself in counseling with the same minister, who had known about his continued molestation of the child for some time. After realizing that the brutalization of her child continued, the woman brought charges against the man and, subsequently, against the minister.

From the many reports of women who have suffered the abuse of themselves or their children, it is apparent that this woman's experience with her church is not unique. In fact, it is quite common for women who seek counsel from their ministers to receive some variation on advice reflecting the minister's belief in a theology of ownership, advice such as,

> Marriage is sacred and you must do whatever you can to hold it together.

> Your husband is the head of your household; do what he tells you and he won't need to resort to violence.

> You must have done something to provoke him; go home and mend your ways so he will not need to behave in this manner.

> All of us must suffer; it makes us more Christ-like. Offer up your suffering to Jesus and he will give you strength to endure.

In most cases, pastors are poorly trained to handle such situations. Yet they are generally unable to admit to their inadequacies, since to do so would require a challenge to the traditional norm. It would particularly challenge norms if the pastor were male and the parishioner female, since they, too, are in the dominant/subordinate dyad. Out of arrogance, embarrassment, ignorance, or feelings of helplessness, pastors often give the impression that violent control of women and children is sometimes a necessary part of family life and must be accepted.

In 1982, the General Board of Global Ministries of the United Methodist Church conducted a study to investigate the presence or absence of domestic violence among its congregants. Gathering data from some forty-seven states, in rural and urban settings, large and small churches, cutting across economic lines, the study found that one in four respondents had been abused by their spouses, and that another one in five respondents had family members or close friends who had been abused. In addition, one in nineteen reported having been abused as children and one in fourteen said they were or had been victims of incest.

This study revealed not only the widespread nature of the problem but the failure of the church to deal with it. Some women documented their attempts to find help from the church:

> While our children were still small and I was being battered, I went to our pastor for counseling. I realized that he meant well, but he laid a heavier burden of guilt on me. His advice was to "pray harder, have more faith, and be grateful for your six fine children."

My pastor's reaction was to call and confront me. I hoped for some help, or at least some consolation and advice, but I received only a lecture on having deceived him and the community into thinking we had a Christian marriage. So in my shock and aloneness, I was given no help. In fact, my pastor contributed to my isolation and shame.[1]

Certainly these pastoral attitudes are not limited to United Methodist clergy. In an article on evangelical church attitudes, Virginia Mollenkott described a woman who reported her husband's sexual abuse of their daughter to their minister. She was told that her husband's behavior must be due to her sexual inadequacies and that she should change her behavior, but must not directly interfere with her husband's actions.[2]

One might wonder at these "pastoral" responses to women in abusive situations. Is it a conscious commitment to a theology of ownership that motivates their interventions? Particularly in the less literalistic churches, one might expect a very different theological stance. Operative theology and espoused theology often diverge; yet the operative pattern makes the most profound statement about genuine commitments and beliefs. Even without a conscious, articulated statement of a belief in male ownership of women ordained by God, the evidence that many pastors act on such a belief is clear.

This belief pervades the whole of our social structure and provides the underpinnings of our human relationships. Without the theology of ownership and its God-given male supremacy, the entire social network would shift radically. Thus the means for maintenance of such a belief system are structured into the social fabric.

MAINTENANCE OF MALE SUPREMACY

As Jean Baker Miller has shown in her classic work *Toward a New Psychology of Women*, the maintenance of a dominant/subordinate social structure depends on the belief by subordinates in the rightness of, not so much their own position, but that of the dominants. The subordinates focus most of their energy on learning as much as possible about the dominants and providing them with what they require.[3] They believe in the authority of dominants because they accept the dominants' superiority, their right to ownership. Miller contends that dominants avoid conflict, since to engage seriously with another might cost them their position.[4] Thus, they use their power in abusive and destructive ways toward subordinates to keep them in their place. Their use of power in this manner is considered legitimate by both their peers and subordinates.

To challenge the authority of men—or even their violent exercise of their authority—to control women would challenge not only the very structure of society but its religious norms as well. It would challenge the legitimacy of a theology of ownership. Belief in the rightness of ownership is necessary for its perpetuation. Men who are consistent abusers claim that their wives belong to them and it is their right to control their wives, even with violence if needed.[5] And incestuous fathers are often surprised to learn that they have broken the law since they believe that sexual access to their children is their right.[6] One legal scholar has noted that sexual abuse is actually not prohibited by law, merely regulated. Since only violence that involves another man's property is prohibited, incest and other forms of domestic violence are often considered within acceptable norms.[7]

Judith Herman maintains that the function of domestic violence is to preserve male supremacy. Speaking specifically of sexual violence, she says that "it is a form of terrorism by which men as a group keep women as a group frightened and submissive. . . . Perpetrators understand intuitively that the purpose of their behavior is to put women in our place and that their behavior will be condoned by other men as long as the victim is a legitimate target."[8] Thus, women live with a fear of men which pervades all of life and which convinces women that their weakness is innate and unchangeable.

Writing in the context of evangelical tradition, Virginia Mollenkott has postulated that the relationship between patriarchy and family violence is symbiotic.[9] Further expanding her contention, I suggest that the relationship between a theology of ownership and family violence is similarly symbiotic. Each feeds and maintains the other and needs the other to exist. Without the potential of violence legitimated by religious tradition which supports it, male supremacy would have little means of perpetuation.

Men who have never engaged in violence joke with their wives that they "rule with an iron fist." Yet their humor carries more truth than they care to admit. Sarcastic jokes about violent control of women are common in the culture. The "humorous" threat of violence appears in the recent revival of the old Jackie Gleason *Honeymooners* show on television, in whose theme song he declares, "One of these days, pow right in the kisser." Without the possibility of violence, the "joke" would not make sense; and without a justifying theology, the potential for violence would have to be controlled.

PHYSICAL AND PSYCHOLOGICAL
HEALTH OF THE OWNED

The consequences of a theology of ownership are dire. It undermines the physical and psychological health of those owned. Even in the most benign situation, women experience a sense of inferiority and lack of self-esteem, both of which have physical as well as psychological consequences. The damage done to women is perhaps best viewed in a situation of domestic violence, which is one manifestation of a theology of ownership.

A common characteristic of abused women is a confused sense of identity.[10] Since, culturally, women's identity is so closely linked to attachment to men, all women must struggle with issues of personal identity formation. Erik Erikson's theory of identity formation fails to describe women's experience adequately, since he sees identity formation as a prerequisite to achieving intimacy.[11] Women have been taught to find their identity first from association with fathers, then from husbands—always in relationship to males who have control over them. Thus, for women, identity and intimacy are always closely intertwined, never separate developmental tasks.

For a woman who suffers abuse, her sense of herself becomes closely tied to her experience of violent control. She may be a high achiever, competent and independent outside the home. With her husband, however, she becomes subject to his violent control, and the sense of self she is able to maintain in other arenas dissolves. She lives in two worlds, with two simultaneous but incongruent experiences of self.

With this confused sense of self, and an ever present fear for her safety (and often that of her children as well), the abused woman must expend all her energy on survival. Whatever gains she may make in developing any sense of positive self-esteem are challenged and usually lost in the atmosphere of fear and intimidation at home. She is used to being criticized, blamed, and punished for her errors. In the cycle of violence characteristic of abusive situations, the abused woman has no opportunity to develop a solid sense of *self*, let alone self-esteem. Her lack of identity and self-esteem becomes further justification for continuation of the cycle—the theology of ownership. Her husband is "responsible" for this poor, weak, incapable creature and must "whip her into shape." Better to beat the woman's body than lose her immortal soul, as a fourteenth-century marriage manual admonishes.

The violence characteristic of ownership poses another block to positive identity formation. As Donald W. Winnicott has described, persons in threatened positions often develop a "false self," an exterior presentation of self designed to please others and to hide the turmoil and pain that characterize the inner self.[12] Though the exterior self may appear intact and highly functional, the inner self testifies to the person her lack of worth. Positive comments and life successes go unheard as she attends to that inner voice that says she is worthless.

Another feeling common to women who are abused or who were sexually violated as children is that they do not own their bodies. They have survived terrifying events by mentally absenting themselves from their bodies and becoming spectators, watching from afar. This dissociation from their physical selves becomes normative, then, for how they view their bodies and further increases their sense of being owned, body and self, by another.

In writing on the task of the pastoral counselor in his recent book *Taking on the Gods*, Merle Jordan urges that the primary question of identity be not, Who am I? but, Whose am I?[13] His admonition that identity cannot be considered outside of this relational question is an attempt to be inclusive of the relational component of self, and as such reflects the theory of such feminist writers as Carol Gilligan and Nancy Chodorow.[14] Yet for women whose experience of being owned—and owned violently—is the primary core of their identity, such a question perpetuates their powerlessness. Perhaps for women, the task is reversed and the primary question should be, Who am I? not, Whose am I?

To add further to their lack of identity, poor self-esteem, and sense of dissociation, victims of abuse often feel that they are isolated and alone. In fact, many such women are kept isolated by their owners, who seem to know that connection with other women might undermine their power. Thus, acts of violence need to be kept secret. If victims try to break out of their isolation by speaking, they are often discredited and shamed.[15]

With problems in identity formation, self-esteem, and control over their own bodies, many women unconsciously resort to their only outlet for pain—their bodies. Psychogenic illnesses are common among abused women, as they actualize their emotional pain in physiological forms. This is not to say that such women imagine physical illnesses; rather, they become physically ill in their efforts to maintain the homeostasis of their lives. Emotional tension, stress, fear, and hurt must be discharged in some manner, and for persons who can find no safe emotional release or means of altering their situations, psychogenic illnesses become that means of release.

Victims of abuse, alone with their pain, and with few personal resources to cope with it, represent the highest cost of a theology of ownership. This destructive pattern cries out for redress. How has the church dealt with this destructive part of its tradition? And how will it?

THE CHURCHES' RESPONSE

Despite the documentation of the breadth of this problem, it remains a "myth" to many pastors. Although 40 percent of battered women report that they went first to their pastors for help, most pastors deny the existence of violence among members of their congregations. The "absence" of the problem represents the failure of the minister to acknowledge its existence and his or her willingness to address it. One participant in a workshop on domestic violence reported that he could not understand why, since he had started the workshop, he had been confronted with three cases of domestic violence in his church. Then he recalled that he had announced from the pulpit a change in his office hours for a few weeks in order to accommodate his participation in the workshop. Apparently, that general announcement was heard as an invitation by some members of his congregation.[16]

The increasing frequency of media reports, special programs, documentaries, and dramas on various forms of domestic violence has forced a few churches to address the problem, mostly in pragmatic denominational ways, such as making pronouncements on the subject of domestic violence. The United Church of Christ issued such a statement in 1983:

> As Christians, believing in the sacredness of God's creation and the equality of women and men, we are called to speak out against the physical and/or sexual abuse of any person. Because women are the primary victims of domestic violence, rape, and sexual harassment this pronouncement calls us to increase our understanding of violence against

women, provide ministry to victims and abusers and work against violence in our society.[17]

The United States Catholic Conference issued a similar, though less directed statement, broadly addressing family violence:

Whether harm is from outside the community or from within the family, the church has a responsibility to those whose well-being is threatened.[18]

And the Episcopal Diocese of Massachusetts has formed a special committee on Women in Crisis to address violence against women. They state:

As Christian people, we are called by God to be co-creators, with God, of a "new heaven, new earth." God has charged humanity with the steward-ship of the world—the natural and societal world—that has been given to us. We must pledge ourselves not to pray only, but also to work, for the coming of the Realm of God proclaimed by Jesus of Nazareth.[19]

These pronouncements are surely significant steps toward acknowl-edging a problem. However, each is directed primarily toward the existence of violence and the need for its eradication. While they call their churches to some sort of action, they do not challenge their institutions' historic stance toward and complicity with the problem. They are pragmatic attempts to confront the problem of domestic violence; yet they are primarily band-aids designed to alleviate a symptom. None of them addresses the underlying theology of owner-ship that enables and sustains a context in which violence is possible.

The roots of this theology—this view of persons that demands a hierarchical structure, a dominant and a subordinate—run deep in the tradition. The use of the Genesis creation story is powerful, but it represents a gross misunderstanding and misuse of Scripture as well as a selective choice of passages. Genesis actually contains two creation stories, representing two different oral traditions which were woven together in the written text. The other version presents male and female as God's creation, fashioned in God's own image. Even literalis-tic readers of the text have an alternate account on which to base their understanding of the nature of men and women. In any case, proof-texting is a futile endeavor since many conflicting claims have been proven by citing opposing biblical texts.

If the Christian tradition is to provide a genuine challenge to violence as a relational norm, some specific changes must occur, changes that incorporate but go far beyond the understanding of biblical text.

First, a firm connection between the personal and the political must be made. Acts of individual violence must be seen for what they are: the sinful violation of relationship and products of a theology that enables and encourages them. Healing must be not only for the individual but between the individual and the communal system that has enabled the abuse. Private pain must become a social, systemic issue and must be healed at its very roots. This means a challenge to theological norms as well as a call to responsibility for violent behavior by members of the Christian community. It means an abandonment of silence as a means of responding to violence and a willingness to confront and name crimes in a public arena. It means that pastors, along with all other care-givers, will have to move out of the study and into the community to demand justice and participate in healing.

Second, the shift from viewing domestic violence as a private issue to seeing it as a public concern requires that the underlying theology of ownership be discarded. It means that one Genesis creation account must be understood for what it is: a culturally bound attempt to explain creation and concurrently to justify the existence of a sinful system of interpersonal relations. It means that public and private interaction of pastors and their congregants can no longer rest on the assumption that subordination is God's will. It means that violence as a means of personal expression must always be labeled sinful and victims of such violence must be protected and supported.

Finally, in place of a theology of ownership, a concept of responsible adulthood must be promulgated. Such a concept challenges the patriarchal notions that pervert personhood. Responsible adults are neither dominants or subordinates but persons who see one another as co-equal and co-responsible in relation to the Creator, and thus are capable of meeting their needs in the context of egalitarian relationships. Responsible adults share power on the basis of capabilities rather than maintaining or assigning it on the basis of random inherent characteristics. Responsible adults define their own worth in terms of their personhood, not on fixed physical characteristics. And they relate to others on the basis of similar ego characteristics.

In a world of responsible adults, violence would be an unacceptable way to deal with one another. That is not to say that violence would never occur. Responsible adults are subject to drives and desires that can lead them at times to act irresponsibly. But such actions would be considered aberrations of adulthood, an unacceptable loss of impulse control, and would be subject to the scrutiny and judgment of religion and society. Such actions would not be normative, so they could be private acts carried on and maintained in secret with the support of theological concepts and social conventions.

Whether or not such a change in theological orientation can occur within the Christian tradition remains to be seen. Surely, the theological bases are there to support such a position. One need only look to the strong female leader models in both the Old and New Testaments to show a precedent for both male and female authority, or to the life and acts of Jesus who relied on women as some of his closest colleagues and who taught an egalitarian gospel of love and peace, or to the many female leaders in the early church and through the centuries who have recently been recovered by feminist scholars. Yet the grip of patriarchy is powerful, and the losses in relinquishing a theology of ownership are many for the owners. However, the losses may be greater still if such a change is not implemented; they may extend to the very loss of the tradition as a normative way of life.

NOTES

1. Peggy Halsey, *Abuse in the Family: Breaking the Church's Silence* (New York: Office of Ministries with Women, General Board of Global Ministry, United Methodist Church, 1982), 4–5.

2. Virginia Mollenkott, "Evangelicalism, Patriarchy, and the Abuse of Children," *Radix* (Jan.–Feb. 1982): 17.

3. Jean Baker Miller, *Toward a New Psychology of Women* (Boston: Beacon Press, 1979), 6.

4. Ibid., 7.

5. Ginny NiCarthy, *Getting Free* (Seattle: Seal Press, 1984), 7.

6. Florence Rush, *The Best Kept Secret: Sexual Abuse of Children* (New York: McGraw-Hill, 1980), 14.

7. Catherine A. MacKinnon, "A Feminism, Marxism, Method, and the State: An Agenda for Theory," in *The Signs Reader* (Chicago: University of Chicago Press, 1983), 86.

8. Judith Herman, *Work in Progress, Sexual Violence* (Wellesley, Mass.: Stone Center, 1984), 4–5.

9. Virginia Mollenkott, "Evangelicalism, Patriarchy and the Abuse of Children," 16.

10. Lenore Walker, *The Battered Woman* (New York: Harper & Row, 1979), 31.

11. Erik Erikson, *Childhood and Society* (New York: W. W. Norton, 1950), 261ff.

12. Donald W. Winnicott, *From Pediatrics to Psychoanalysis* (New York: Basic Books, 1975).

13. Merle Jordan, *Taking on the Gods* (Nashville: Abingdon Press, 1986), 22.

14. See Carol Gilligan, *In a Different Voice* (Cambridge: Harvard University Press, 1982); and Nancy Chodorow, *The Reproduction of Mothering: Psychoanalysis and the Sociology of Gender* (Berkeley and Los Angeles: University of California Press, 1978).

15. Herman, *Work in Progress*, 4.

16. Marie Fortune, "Domestic Violence and Theological Education" (conference in San Antonio, Texas, 1985).

17. Statement of the United Church of Christ at the Fourteenth General Synod, 1982.

18. Statement of the United States Catholic Conference of Bishops, Washington, D.C., 1984.

19. *Women in Crisis Bulletin* (Boston: The Episcopal Diocese of Massachusetts, 1985).

8

The Fallacy of
Individualism and
Reasonable Violence Against Women

POLLY YOUNG-EISENDRATH / DEMARIS WEHR

Promising a deep and effective knowledge of the natural world, Descartes' practical philosophy held out the great hope that, instead of victims, we may become masters and possessors, not only of nature, but of our own natures also.

—J. Shotter, *Social Accountability and Selfhood*

I'm not always comfortable with my own sexuality because I can feel very vulnerable when I'm making love. It's a bit crazy, I suppose, because in sex is when I'm experiencing the essence of my manhood and also when I can feel the most frightened about it—like I'm not my own man, or I could lose myself, or something like that.

—L. Rubin, *Intimate Strangers*

MENTAL SEPARATISM AND THE FALLACY
OF INDIVIDUALISM

Since the seventeenth century, in reflecting on ourselves, we have heeded the "voice of reason." Modern philosophy and psychology began with the work of René Descartes as he formulated a rational-empirical method for validating the truth of science and introspective enlightenment. Descartes' methods are still far more than mere historical records for Western society, which emphasizes the ideals of rational freedom. Descartes articulates our cultural preferences for individualism, the superiority of rational thought, and the skepticism of the informed, who doubt the immediacy of their experiences. Descartes is not dead. It seems appropriate, then, to allow him a few words.

I resolved . . . to speak only of what would happen in a new world, if God were to create, somewhere in imaginary space, enough matter to compose it, and if *He* were to agitate diversely and confusedly the different parts of this matter, so that *he* created a chaos as disordered as the poets could ever imagine, and afterwards did no more than to lend *his* usual preserving action to nature, and let *her* act according to *his* established laws.[1]

Through the practical methods of Descartes' metaphysics, he could imagine a world that would permit him to study the laws of God. Nature would be brought under the control of man in such a way that this control would be, in principle, according to the laws of God. Descartes described an ideal dialogue between God and man. Through such dialogue, God's laws would become accessible and reveal an increasingly comprehensive explanation of the relationship of God to men and men to God. Through knowing the dialogue of God and man, Descartes fashioned a worldview.

A worldview is a map or template that presents the "bigger picture" or the foundational guidelines for truth and reality. People live within worldviews and reproduce explanatory concepts that are consensually validated according to their shared worldviews. Cartesian worldviews have captivated Western culture and emphasize a repetitive theme in patriarchy: the superiority of doubt and distancing in knowing oneself and the world. This method of knowing, this epistemology, has many consequences in terms of both what we know and who knows it. Through conversations and cultural records, dominant men have shaped cultural accounts of ideal selves that have depicted a theme of "mastery over," using doubt, distancing, and debate, among other strategies. For the most part, patriarchal accounts of ideal selves and the daily activities that unite men in their worldviews have excluded diverse and variant subjectivities.

Contemporary Western worldviews have tended to be organized by dichotomy or oppositions: mind/body, human/divine, man/nature, inner/outer, fantasy/reality, science/art, reason/emotion, subject/object. One pole of the dichotomy may be privileged, or the two may be understood to be in dynamic interaction; but whatever the content of the opposition, *woman* has been excluded as a valid pole of tension. When we consider the myriad varieties of these oppositions—including even masculine/feminine—we are startled to discover that we have no ideal model, no oppositional tension, for the relationship of man and woman in standard patriarchal worldviews. The "feminine" in the masculine/feminine dichotomy does not represent the voice of woman. Woman has no place, no articulated position, in the reality of most of our recorded knowledge. She is "off the record." Consequently, her ideas and concerns are frequently considered trivial and insignificant. (Even amidst our contemporary projects of female epistemology and ontology, the "women's movement" remains stubbornly insignificant for many people, both female and male.) Because she is non-signed and absent from our worldviews, because she is subsumed under the concept of *human nature* without a valid subjectivity of her own, the achievements and losses of women are easily forgotten.

Abuses of women's bodies, property, and integrity are difficult to conceive as rational problems of a principled morality even in Western culture today. Because the female person is invisible, silent, without her own subjectivity, her experiences can be "objectified" by male observers. Her suffering is stubbornly inconsequential in spite of the humane intentions of many political and legal attempts to include her under the rubric of "human welfare."

Since the female person has not been part of the Western worldview, and since her subjectivity is unrecorded, many women are reticent to speak their experiences. Women's accounts, especially of suffering and abuse, are frequently perceived as "incredible" and unbelievable, even to themselves.

Moreover, some hard-core psychological beliefs and root metaphors hold sway over the depiction of lived realities. These metaphors are the vehicles for speech in assembling *any* text of the personal world, as told by female or male persons. Reality testing, validating, and truth telling do not arise directly from observations, intuitions, or experiences. Rather, reality is constructed among people according to the guidelines of their worldview and root metaphors. As Willis Overton says of the scientific endeavors of contemporary "normal science":

> Metaphysical propositions, as they may constitute the hard core of scientific research programs, are not . . . simply idle psychological or sociological curiosities, rather they are essential components of scientific activity. They exert a formative influence on lower levels and give meaning to the theoretical concepts of specific theories. . . . Another characteristic of the hard core is that it is not open to falsification. That is, the hard core is irrefutable.[2]

One particular root metaphor concerns us here: the individual mind as a separate mental space. Although Descartes was not the author of autonomous individuality, his famous statement, "I think, therefore I am," expresses it well. The conceptual error of imagining a person to be a discrete, self-generating individual (a body giving rise to a mind, or a mind housed in a body) is what we call the *fallacy of individualism*. This error has promoted debate and fostered major questions in psychological, philosophical, and theological reasoning in both ordinary and academic worldviews in Western culture for four centuries. Whether the Mind is embodied or disembodied, it is perceived as "contained" within a unit (e.g., a brain, a black box, a body) under the control of a separate individual. The individual, the subject or "I," is the best avenue of its own reflection; it can know itself and become objectified. Not only does this mean that "man has dominion over his own nature," but also that the isolated individual exists. The existence of an isolated individual is absurd although we speak as though it were possible all of the time. At the present time the metaphors of mental separatism continue to prevail in all cultural arenas that have been influenced by Cartesian thought.

Because we have no ideals for dependence and community in the mature articulation of self, we may be dumbfounded at the prospect of cross-gender dialogue and empathy. Each gender has contained, birthed, supported, and described the other over eons of time, but we have created no ideal model for our relationship. As I said, a major barrier in this project is that Woman has not been admitted to reality in Western culture. In her absence we have been unable to recognize our continued dependence on each other over the life span not only for supportive and survival resources but also for understanding and believing ourselves.

In the shadow of this problem, we have erected and subscribed to many psychological theories, usually organized by the root metaphor of the mind as a spatial place. Female experiences and realities have been objectified by male observers, cast into an "otherness" that is alien, exotic, remote, subversive, submissive, or silent. Their validity cannot inherently make sense because the independent male thinker reveals the female person as unknown, as the hated and envied residue of his *rational freedom*.

Within the past decade and a half, we have witnessed the attempts of many feminist theorists and practitioners to articulate new models of female experience that include new meanings and conversations. Two major belief systems stand in the way of women securely placing our own metaphors of female subjectivity into our language and culture: (1) the continuing belief that men control the knowledge necessary to direct women's lives as they exist within patriarchal cultures; and (2) the belief that men control the major resources on which humankind depends. Jean Lipman-Blumen assumes that these beliefs dominate and hamper us in our analyses of gender roles and power.[3] Feminist analyses of resources, vitality, agency, and ideals of female persons must provide persuasive counterpositions in order to increase the possibility and ease of women to speak for themselves. Indeed, women have begun to do this, offering guidelines specifically for constructing the validity of female experience (within patriarchy) in order to retrieve female authority.[4]

Here we try to further these attempts by exploring a feminist understanding of violence against women. In contrast to other modes of analysis that have adhered to mental separatism in attempting to understand such abuse, we would like to reveal the fallacy of individualism in current rationalizations of violence against girls and women. We have chosen two forms of violence that continue daily in our free North American societies without arousing outrage in the public at large; that, in fact, have gone practically unnoticed over eons of time within patriarchy: prostitution and the battering of girls and women. We believe that a reformulation of these actions, avoiding the entrapments of individualism and mental separatism, can restore the validity of female experience to both female and male persons so that we can recognize that such violent abuse of female people is not simply a moral outrage, but is also a complete and utter absurdity in terms of the interdependence of personal beings.

PERSONS AND SELVES

A person is an embodied being who is both a point of view (mentality, perception) *and* a point of action (movement, agency). Through our relationships with other persons, we (human beings) become person-alities. P. F. Strawson, John MacMurray, and Rom Harre have provided philosophical and psychological groundwork for our definition of "persons" as primary beings of a "first order" in our experience, publicly visible and "endowed with all kinds of powers and capacities for public, meaningful action."[5] There is no occasion under any circumstances in which a person is a mind or body. In ongoing communications with persons, from birth to death, we inhabit a shared intelligence that permits us to be knowers and doers. Originally each of us is contained within a female person and then is gradually encompassed by a broader and broader circle of other persons. No knowledge or experience of personal being is first learned alone and then shared with others. In order to have experiences at all we need the resources, reflections, and definitions of others. Personal being is originally and continuously a shared existence.

A "self" is secondarily acquired within a culture of persons. Self, from our perspective, is a construct or belief system about individual subjectivity. The construct of self and the experience of subjectivity take on meanings within the culture in which one develops as a person. Beliefs about self determine how persons relate to each other and to their environment. As Harre says, "A person is a being who has learned a theory, in terms of which his or her experience is ordered."[6] The characteristics of our theories of subjectivity, our self-theories, are central both to our attitudes toward our lived lives, and to our assumptions about our own person-alities.

In North American society, beliefs about self include an array of ideals in support of individual autonomy. We are a society of unique, self-reflective, independent individuals—in our own regard. Not only have we created epistemologies and ontologies whose root metaphor is mental separatism, but we have also founded our morality on assumptions of separate individual freedom and responsibility.

FEMALE SELVES

How does female gender enter into the creation of independent selves? Because female people are broadly considered less than or inferior to complete male people, women regularly surrender the validity of their own truths in the face of challenges by men and others perceived to be powerful. The idea that female means inferior is a hardcore belief that has been part of the modern worldview as reflected in psychological, philosophical, literary, and theological records. Female persons necessarily participate in everyday conversations in which the given worldview includes the assumption of female inferiority and inadequacy. Inevitably they arrive at adulthood with feelings and significant beliefs about their own inferiority. These are not just occasional or transitory ideas, but firm convictions of the particular inferiority of body, attractiveness, nurturance, or intelligence that have been built into the construction of the female self.

Female persons will strive to validate theories of subjective inferiority in a patriarchal society such as ours. In order to participate in the social order and to be considered rightful persons, girls and women have to surrender the authority of their own truth, beauty, and goodness. They replace this authority with self-theories of inadequacy. Their willingness to identify in some way with the theory of inferiority of female self is a fact of survival. Such identities are attributed and sustained in ongoing conversations in which both the social context (i.e., verbal and nonverbal communications) and the hard-core beliefs have been shaped by the assumption that female persons lack *something*. When girls and women witness their inability to fill decision-making and status-holding positions, they frequently take this as evidence of the theory of their individual inferiority and the general devaluation of what they have produced. According to the theory of inferiority of the female self, a woman usually asks herself, What is wrong with *me*?

THE DOUBLE BIND OF
FEMALE SELVES

Until a woman is offered a feminist explanation for her felt condition of personal inferiority, she is necessarily in a double bind about her gender and her status as an independent adult. In patriarchal society we are constantly subjected to tacit and explicit assumptions of male superiority. There is much empirical evidence of the collective prejudice we share about gender identities.[7] American women are expected to be weaker, less competent, and more emotionally expressive than their male counterparts. Moreover, the portrait of the ideal woman includes a greater degree of passive dependence than does that of the healthy adult, when gender is not specified for the latter. Personal responsibility and self-determination of a healthy adult—in our society so essential for the democratic vision of free will—are directly in conflict with ideals for female gender in adulthood. If a woman behaves as a healthy adult, she will be criticized for being unwomanly; conversely, if she behaves as an ideal feminine woman, she will be considered childlike or worse, even mentally incompetent.

This double bind of female authority is unavoidable in a society that predicates the validity of the individual self on the very attributes that the female is assumed to have considerably less of than the ideal kind or amount. The categories of self-determination, which permit the acceptance of a person as an adult in our social order, are not generally expected to be fulfilled by individual women.

Many women in North America oppose these stereotypes of the ideal woman and openly espouse beliefs of adequacy, competence, and authority in themselves. Unfortunately, they cannot easily escape the double bind of female authority because it is part and parcel of our social order. Consequently, authoritative and insistent women are frequently labeled and described as *compensating* for their inferior position. They may be described as too masculine, too controlling, too emotional, too intellectual, or just too much. In many public arenas, insistent women experience great distress when they follow their own desires and defend their beliefs. As Harre points out, the legitimacy of being a person (especially the right to contribute to conversations and cultural records) is limited by the right to occupy time and space in the ongoing shared reality and worldview.[8] This contingent right is guarded by a consensual validation of people's worth, bound by social roles, status, race, and gender.

Authoritative women frequently find themselves in a mediated position. What they are saying or offering is undermined because they have assumed a posture of authority; they may be seen and not heard because their position is considered "compensatory." The personal existence of such women is threatened at these moments and they often get the impression that they are "doing something wrong." Rather than suffer emotional turmoil or abandon their rights to participate in the consensual validity of dialogue, they tend to accept explanations that expose their theological inferiority. They may even see themselves as too controlling, too manipulative, too dominating.

Authoritative women fall prey to evaluating themselves in terms of a negative subjectivity, an inferior self or personality. Frequently they even come to conceive of their backgrounds, characteristics, attitudes, and traits as inherently problematic. Until such a woman is released from the double bind of female self, she will be prone to constructing herself as inferior although she subscribes to a broadly different theory about women.

Women who accept the less-than orientation to their gender have a different fate. They are usually better accepted within the social order in terms of their valid self-presentations. They are perceived as valid persons under the conditions of their oppression, but they experience the validity of these conditions as their own inherent weaknesses (e.g., inferior intellects) and childlikeness. Many syndromes of mental illness are characterized by exaggerated pictures of stereotyped femininity: depression, dependent personality, hysteria, phobia, bulimia, anorexia, and aspects of borderline personality disorder are but a few examples. When feminine-identified women seek help at public and private facilities for mental health, they risk being labeled into these categories precisely because they have identified with the ideal characteristics of the inferior gender.

REASONABLE VIOLENCE AGAINST WOMEN

A summary of conclusions from a study of rape tolerance among prisoners, university students, and adolescents emphasize that "those who tolerated rape tended to perceive women as sex objects and to condone male dominance of women. This relationship was substantial among both females and males. Rape tolerance thus had the same attitudinal correlates among women and men."[9]

The perception of Other as *object*—as well as the consequent objectification of the Other—is a hard-core belief undergirding many versions of rational individualism. Female persons and female sexuality are conceived as objects for rational and political control, dominance, and analysis. In masculinist systems of thought from medicine to androcentric psychologies to cinematography and theology, the female is dreaded, idealized, envied, and occulted. Her body and sexuality become the objects of male speculation and domination in proportion to the degree she is without valid subjectivity, assumed to be alien and insignificant to male identity concerns.

Sunder L. Gilman, in his study of the pathological significance of gender and race, speculates that different anatomical structures are the *signs* that permit us to project onto the Other our own fears of losing self-control.

> It is thus the innate fear of the Other's different anatomy which lies behind the synthesis of images. The Other's pathology is revealed in her anatomy, and the black and the prostitute are both bearers of the stigmata. . . . The "white *man's* burden," his sexuality and its control, is displaced into the need to control the sexuality of the Other, the Other as sexualized female.[10]

Both the idealized version of female Other—the *madonna*—and the devalued version—the *whore*—are male stereotypes introduced into patriarchy through men's speculations and analyses of female persons. The madonna and the whore belong to male psychology, displaced onto the female person as object, and are not indigenous to female psychology.

As Kathleen Barry points out in her comprehensive review of female prostitution, "Male dominance reduces women to a lower status, holding them in low regard, and at the same time it makes women the objects of men's personal need for love, romance, and sex. The oppressors of women carry the unique responsibility of masculinist values to both love and hate women."[11]

Idealization, hatred, and envy are aspects of infantile relationships with parenting figures, as many psychologists have pointed out. Early human development includes images of great emotional power and resources in which the parental Other is imagined to be both Great and Terrible. The absolute dependence of infancy contributes to the experiences of the mythical Big Ones who seem to the child to sustain and control life.

Later development, in childhood and adolescence, permits the recognition of equality and reciprocity based on trust, through relating to peers in mutual exchanges. The translation of equality and reciprocity into understanding authority figures in adulthood is characteristic of successful development in our society. Idealization, hatred, and envy are not effective components of ordinary relationships among adults. Yet these infantile emotional states are much in evidence in the objectification of the female person; they are rationalized through hard-core beliefs in individual freedom and mental separatism within our North American society.

RATIONALIZED BATTERING OF WOMEN AND GIRLS

The combined effects of mental separatism, individual freedom, and infantile emotional states have led to widespread masculinist permission for men to dominate women based on stereotypes. This permission has included the right to violate the bodies of female persons in order to keep them "under control" or to retaliate for wounded feelings. As Barry says,

Wife-beaters exemplify men who contain the mandate to both love and hate women within one relationship. Other men who do not want to inflict contempt, disgust, and hatred on their loved one may still need to act it out. Prostitution provides that opportunity.[12]

Battering and prostitution are thus united as violent ways of using the objectified female body to express infantile emotional states. That we in North America continue to rationalize and permit violent abuses of women seems to indicate that we, both female and male persons, share root metaphors and hard-core beliefs that make such abuses reasonable, that is, thinkable.

In Leonore Walker's accounts of female battering, she repeatedly shows how the belief systems held by the participants in a battering relationship contribute to their enduring participation.[13] These beliefs tend to express a single desire: to master another person's experience as if it were one's own. Polly Young-Eisendrath and Florence Wiedemann have traced the ways in which women in general are unable to validate their experiences in patriarchy, unable until and if they come into contact with a female epistemology that offers new worldviews.[14] Our analysis of person, self, and gender in this essay touched on the main issues of the double bind of female authority. Walker's studies of women coping with abusive men poignantly reveal the tendency to invalidate female (even one's own) claims to truth. A typical example is Alice's story about Mike, the initial version of which ends as follows:

> Apparently, when Mike pushed me into the stove and maybe when he was stomping on me with his feet, my kidneys were damaged. As soon as they got me to the hospital, they could barely find my pulse, and they knew there was internal bleeding. They rushed me into emergency surgery and had to remove one kidney. . . . I don't know what happened. I don't know how it got so bad. It just seems like it's all one great big nightmare. I just don't know what I'll do. How can anyone so kind and gentle like Mike, that I could love so much and who could love me so much, do this to me?[15]

More develops in Alice's story as Mike tries to make amends after the battering incident. He brings flowers, apologizes, idealizes, and promises, all to convince her that he "really loves" her and that she should not leave him. He asserts that the battering was not "his fault" and that he can repair the damages done to Alice. He proposes that they take a cruise together when she gets out of the hospital.

Walker visits Alice again in the hospital, after she has been thus persuaded by Mike. Now Alice reports the following about the battering circumstances:

I'm really not sure how the whole incident happened. Perhaps it was my fault. Mike says he really didn't throw me against the stove. He just pushed at me and I fell and hit the stove. I really believe him. He couldn't have wanted to hurt me as badly as I was hurt. It really must have been an accident.[16]

How can we—with Walker's assistance—explain the shift in Alice's beliefs about Mike's involvement, a shift from his "stomping" on her with his feet to the notion that perhaps it was her fault?

From Walker's analysis, we can assume that Alice has low self-esteem, accepts the traditional masculinist stereotypes about women's place and roles, and is willing to believe that she is at fault for others' actions. Although Walker provides complete and graphic evidence of the reproduction of patriarchal stereotypes in her accounts of battering, she does not examine the belief systems that permit both battered and battering persons to rationalize the violence. Clearly the terror and physical intimidation of battering itself are reasons enough for Alice to become docile and submissive in the face of potentially further attacks, but Walker contends that women like Alice *are* competent to change their environments and protect themselves. Frequently they do not *want* to do so. They believe their male partners' promises and explanations over and above their own experiences. They validate the males' accounts of reality over against their own.

We conclude, from our perspective, that Alice (like many of us) maintains her ability to be validated as a person by collecting evidence of her own inadequacy. She reassures herself that the prevailing male assertions and stereotypes of her "irritating" and "overwhelming" behavior are true because if she does otherwise, she has no basis for reality—no worldview. Hence she would have no right to occupy time and space in the normal conversations of everyday life.

There is no great leap from Alice's trivializing of her suffering to the invalidity assigned by other women to their complaints about battering and abuse. The rubric of "domestic violence" is a rationalized term for typical occasions of male persons—husbands, fathers, brothers, sons—inflicting aggressive violence on female persons as a method of problem-solving in conflict. Barry cites the statistic that "in one year some 1.8 million wives are beaten by their husbands" from estimates in the 1970s in the United States.[17] Outrageous statistics and reports of violence against girls and women have become a norm in many patriarchal societies and yet few moral people are outraged. Why?

Four conditions persist that support rationalization of expressed threats and aggression against female persons:

1. masculinist explanations of human behavior that exclude or repress the fact of absolute dependence in human life;
2. gender stereotypes that function, as explained above, to encourage girls and women to construct inadequate selves and to gather evidence of their continued inadequacy in their experiences of individual subjectivity;
3. cultural permissions afforded to male persons (by virtue of their gender) to express aggression and infantile impulses within their idealization, hatred, and envy of female persons;
4. the fear experienced by girls and women who are the "objects" of such expressed aggression.

As Barry has pointed out, theories linked to battering and abuse of girls and women frequently conclude that "violence breeds violence" as though such an explanation could replace the responsibility that must be taken by those who enact aggression. This kind of explanation becomes a cultural permission that is afforded to male persons to continue to batter. As Barry says, "It is not necessarily violence that breeds violence. It is the fact that sexually abusive men—pimps, husbands, or fathers—many of whom learn violence at an early age as a means of problem solving, still receive sanction for their behavior."[18]

Arguments that rationalize violent abuse of another person are always rooted in hard-core beliefs of mental separatism and autonomous individualism. Usually the arguments are predicated on one or more of the following ideas: some people choose (pornography, prostitution, battering); some people need (to blow up, to let out steam); it is natural that men want to dominate women because men have greater physical strength and/or testosterone (the "aggressive hormone"). Such arguments about the "rights" of men are usually a blend of individualism (i.e., "people have the right to choose") and infantile emotions (e.g., "men are just naturally aggressive and mean because of their hormones"). These rationalizations become social sanctions for male persons to abandon control of infantile impulses.

In general, we expect adults to control such impulses and most of the time they do. For example, impulses to express murderous threats to strangers, to urinate and defecate in public, or to remove one's clothing in public are generally effectively controlled through the local moral order and public scrutiny.

Public scrutiny and punishment have not been directed against acts of battering, especially when they are considered to be "domestic violence." Moreover, theological explanations for battering have tended to reproduce some form of mental separatism and individualism so as to assume that individual men are internally dominated by thoughts, impulses, needs, and desires that are exclusively male—and uncontrollable in the face of *female persons*. Men are almost *expected* to behave in an infantile manner under certain circumstances involving female persons. Women—with clearly the same infantile impulses of idealization, hatred, and envy—are expected to contain their aggressive impulses and, largely, they do.

RATIONALIZED PROSTITUTION OF
THE FEMALE PERSON

Prostitution is the ultimate expression of hatred and envy of the female body by male persons. Exploited as an object for use, a commodity for sale, and a form of entertainment or sporting activity (similar to the abuse of natural terrains), prostitution exemplifies the status of women in patriarchal societies. Social attitudes that tolerate the enslavement and abuse of female persons are clearly an illustration of male individualism.

Barry says, "In light of the practice of domestic slavery that exploits Third World women, and the protective United States laws that support these practices, it is not surprising to find the United Nations acting as an international brotherhood to protect its own. It will not interfere with its member nations' abusive practices toward women when its officials are themselves privately carrying out these practices."[19] Arguments about prostitution tend to rationalize male dominance and control in terms of "natural" dominance-submission instincts. Inevitably, these lead to circular arguments that rationalize slavery as a basic human condition, especially female sexual slavery. As Barry writes,

> Curiously, when we discuss prostitution internationally, the arguments of cultural relativism are silenced and cultural universals are asserted. The result is that the sexual slavery practiced within the family is protected and defended by one set of standards—those based on family privacy and cultural uniqueness—while sexual slavery in brothels and through pimps is supported by the opposite standard, the cultural universal that is based

on the assumption that all men in all cultures through all time must have access to prostitutes.[20]

When the female person has been treated as a body and a sexual object there emerges a dimension of circularity in arguments based on the fallacy of individualism: some female persons supposedly choose prostitution as a way of life, and so should not be barred from pursuing their chosen career. Obviously this line of reasoning neglects the context in which a female person develops in such a way as to choose freely to be treated as an object, a piece of flesh, in exchange for economic supports. Even if there are such cases of girls and women who choose freely—and this is a major question from the perspective of Barry's study that maintains that all prostitutes have been initiated into the abuse of their bodies by pimps or other men, such as their caretakers in childhood—then we must question the context that creates oneself as an object, rather than support the existence of such a context according to the fallacy of individualism.

Barry pursues the question of context and development in American society. She focuses on the idea of arrested sexual development in male persons as her critical concern. "Learned, impulsive, uncontrollable adolescent male sex drive has become for many men the mode of their adult sexual behavior. It is *arrested sexual development*, which stems from a sexuality that has not grown beyond what was acted out at age 12, 13 or 14."[21] The idealizing of sex as power, autonomy, and control over others is notably the problem of American males:

> From the adolescent social situation . . . boys learn that sex is power. They act—the other must react. . . . They find that the female object they choose for sexual release cannot say no, or that even saying no, she really means yes.[22]

The critical element here is the complete alienation of the Other, the disregard for the female experience—her words, her validity, her subjectivity. When the resistance of the Other is reduced to the imaginings of the self—"even saying no, she really means yes"—the Other has been eradicated. What remains to validate the male position is the fallacy of individualism, the rationalization of mental separatism: "I think, therefore I am."

It is no surprise that female persons cannot individually overcome the eradication of their validity and subjectivity. They are also the product of patriarchal worldviews. Until they have securely adopted alternate paradigms, new root metaphors, and hard-core beliefs about the adequacy of female gender and experience, they will be themselves vulnerable to validating—and even enacting—masculinist rationales for female sexual slavery.

ALTERNATE PARADIGMS: SIGNS OF A SHARED EXISTENCE

Most adults in our society would be loath to call themselves "dependent" and have no adequate language to express a mature, differentiated dependence. Existing within the hard-core belief of personal freedom and the fallacy of individualism, adults typically speak only about their rights to be free agents and unique originators.

From our perspective, the "human body" is a social group characterized by attached others whose resistances and reflections give groundwork to identity: earliest, the parents and siblings, then the peers and friends, our partners and children, the community and our mentors, and, finally, the dead whom we gradually join.

The fallacy of individualism and ideals of mental separatism are thoroughly at odds with the shared nature of human existence. The authority of masculine supremacy—the belief that some men should rule our knowledge systems because they are better equipped, more resourceful, or have our best interests in mind—has blended with mental separatism to give the impression that knowledge systems are devised by a few *originators*. Granting privilege to the thoughts of a few particular men ("geniuses in their own right," e.g., Newton, Freud, Darwin, Einstein) has led us to believe that knowledge arrives in a vacuum of introspection or solitary investigations. How differently might we understand the discoveries of these men if the record had included the contributions of the women, children, servants, neighbors, and friends as the work proceeded? Perhaps we would now have the epistemological tools to understand the shaping of new ideas through communications, beliefs, root metaphors, and shared activities of groups of attached people.

New models of dependent relating, dependent co-origination, and attachment bonds are beginning to contribute to alternate paradigms for understanding personal being. Feminists invite us especially to use the records we have on hand to retrieve what has been hidden from our view, to reveal what has been obscured in patriarchal record keeping: the validity of female voice and vision. In claiming the validity of our continuing experiences, we can peer into the shadows of contemporary patriarchy and begin to think in new forms.

John Bowlby's extensive study of attachment bonds between parents and infants introduces another pathway to a new paradigm, in which dependence is recognized as the key to survival among all persons. Bowlby asserts the explanatory power of "relational propositions" in understanding the development of personality.[23] He emphasizes the epistemological contribution made by such propositions as they overtake the fallacy of individualism in psychologies of infancy: "that emotionally significant bonds between individuals have basic survival functions and therefore a primary status" and "that in order for the systems to operate efficiently, each partner builds in his (*sic*) mind working models of self and other, and of the patterns of interaction that have developed between. . . ."[24] Although Bowlby's language is still limited by root metaphors of the "individual mind," his theory and research are attempts to highlight relational units as the stuff of personality.

British object relations theorist W. Ronald Fairbairn first coined the term "mature dependence" in his explorations of "schizoid" disturbances. He provides a characterization of healthy personality development that moves from an "infantile dependence," through "quasi-independence" (hypervigilance about one's separateness), to "mature dependence," a recognition of the nature of giving-taking as the groundwork for adult functioning.[25] Although Fairbairn uses the unfortunate language of Freudian object relations theory (i.e., in speaking about persons as "objects" and about feelings as "cathexes"), he invites feminists to review our current status in patriarchy in terms of "infantile dependence" and "quasi-independence." Earlier in this essay, we tried to show how both the fallacy of individualism (quasi-independence) and infantile impulses (infantile dependence) contribute to rationalizing abuses of female persons.

Luce Irigaray provides a complete review of the cultural position of the female person within patriarchy in her analyses of the Cartesian *cogito* and its contribution to mental separatism.[26] Irigaray especially stresses the effects of critical philosophy on the development of culture, highlighting the methods of doubt and suspicion used by such philosophy. Here is a sample of her descriptions of the effects of mental separatism on our understanding of consciousness:

This "I" exists over and above the day-to-day material of perception and is assured of being throughout everything and beyond everything. Whatever else, other than itself, may happen . . . Saying "no" to everything is the crucial way to be assured that one is really [like] oneself. Otherwise, there will always be doubts about what relates to the self and what to the other. About the reflections others might have in the self, and the self in the Other.[27]

The generalized method Irigaray discovers in Descartes is hyperbolic doubt.

The systematic doubting of all perceptions and experiences, validating only those arising from one's own thoughts, leads to the distortion we have been describing as the fallacy of individualism. Irigaray asserts further that the method of hyperbolic doubt also undergirds the abuse of female persons. By separating and distancing oneself from one's context (bonded relationships) and denying one's dependence, a male person increases his fear of relationship and of the mystery of being. From Irigaray's perspective, the mystery of being includes the primary recognition of *matrix*, the female person and her body, as the origin and the homeplace of human life. In order to believe in his separate existence, a man empties the reality of (M)Other through doubts and suspicions. His obsessive self-reflections eventually deprive the female Other of her intrinsic worth and value. "It is . . . by distance and separation that he will affirm his self-identity."[28] Having established himself as separate—by emptying the female of her worth—the male person now assumes she is needy, inadequate, and incomplete. Ultimately, this perception leads him (back) to infantile fear and rage because the (M)Other who is now "deprived of everything" must want "to take possession of everything."[29]

The circularity of this reasoning is similar to rationalization of battering and prostitution. The denial of dependence and the devaluing of female worth contribute directly to abusive violence against female persons. When we stop our obsessive self-reflections and quiet our doubts, we discover immediately the matrix of personal being. It is a permanent interactive shared relationship, even "psychological symbiosis . . . in the course of which one supplements the psychological attributes of the other."[30] To consider dependence as primary to all personal being—rational and emotional, physical and psychological—we claim the grounds of our experience beyond the confines of self-reflection. We recognize that the ground of being is inside another person from whom we gradually differentiate through a dependent relationship. Within this infantile dependence we discriminate the basis of cognition in structure (comfort/discomfort, good/bad, self/other) and language (the caretakers who "speak us" before we can speak). Then we take on our personal projects of constituting a secure self-other experience in the collusion of body-psyche images. These distinctions are not wholly complete until we recognize *both* self and other as *continuous* and *ambivalent*. In other words, we finally secure a personal being (being a person-among-persons) by making the same attributions of continuity and ambivalence to self and other (called "object constancy" within object relations theory).

Such a quasi-independence is a more differentiated state of symbiosis. Fairbairn would regard this step as the "exteriorizing" of the Other who had previously been incorporated into oneself. We regard the physical birth of the infant as the exteriorization of the "incorporated" being, and thus the first step in differentiation. In this way, we will never fall back to self-reflection as reality and origin: "I think, therefore I am." Rather, our version might be, "I have lived inside another person, so I am a person."

Throughout the life span, a mature person fluctuates between taking and giving, supplementing and being sustained by the attributes of the Other. This is roughly what Fairbairn means by "mature dependence" when one's gratitude is conscious. There is no point in the entire lifespan when the imagination even exists in complete solitude. It is not the completion of one's own thoughts that indicates rationality, for example, but rather the reflections from other persons that one has followed the rules for rational discourse.

In order to achieve a state of mature dependence, persons must become empathic with each other. Empathy, we believe, is a developmental achievement that blends the subjectivity of intuition with the objectivity of rationality. It is an ability to infer accurately another person's worldview, another person's validity. It is different from fusion, projection, and sympathy, but probably develops from these. In order to be empathic, a person must (1) recognize the central importance of dependence to human existence on a continuous basis; (2) communicate within a differentiated understanding of psychological dependence; and (3) be able to tolerate the differences and the resistances of the Other, within a primary state of bondedness, so that the self can be distinguished from the other—authenticity from distortion.

The outcome of empathic relating is true compassion, the ability to recognize another's suffering and to relieve it.

Through dependence, attachment, and compassion we come to know ourselves by knowing others. It is only possible to understand and know one's experiences through encountering the reflections and resistances of others. Only through a reevaluation of what has been denied in ourselves, and projected into others, can we claim the responsibility for our own actions. We clarify our intentions, delineate our conscious choices, and make the ground of our personal being through our bonded relationships.

Although we cannot detail the entire scope of personal being through dependence, we can say in general that movement over the life span is from action to symbol, from impulse to language, from habit to awareness. Such movement is sustained through dependent relationships with others. As people age in the second half of the life span, they become increasingly aware of the meaning of dependence and attachment through loss, limitation, and death.

Within our model of mature dependence, it is immediately clear that violent abuse of the Other is unthinkable. To hinder or eradicate the subjectivity of the Other is to eliminate oneself. To oppress and devalue the Other is to lose one's hope and spirit. Abusive violence is absurd when the grounds of personal being are recognized as fundamentally shared.

In a recent article, Carol Turkington reports that sexual aggression and abuse are "anything but rare" and that attitudes supporting them are also common.[31] "In one study, up to 60 percent of 'normal' American men said they might force a woman to commit sexual acts against her will if they could get away with it. When the phrase 'commit sexual acts' was changed to the loaded term 'rape,' about 20 percent of the subjects still said they might commit such an act if they wouldn't be found out."[32] From the point of view of mature dependence "not being found out" is absurd, crazy. Such sexual actions are between two or more persons; both of them typically "know" they are involved. Moreover, the distortions that arise in the subject of the abuse are concretized in actions, thoughts, habits, and identity. They are inescapable, as much as are those of the abused.

Without an attitude of compassion and a valuing of dependence, people are capable of gross violations of the terms of their existence on this planet. We are presently captured by our own ideals of mental separatism and the fallacy of individualism in such a way that we frequently cannot distinguish our survival from our extinction. Male dominance of female persons, the abuse of any person, and the denial of our dependence are unthinkable violations of our existence. We hope that the revaluing of female experience and the validation of attachment as the basis of personal being will help us to remember the limited control and the limitless dependence that characterize our species.

NOTES

1. René Descartes, *Discourse on Method and Other Writings*, trans. with introduction by F. E. Sutcliffe (Harmondsworth, Eng.: Penguin Books, 1968), 62. Emphasis added.

2. W. Overton, "Worldviews and Their Influence on Psychological Theory and Research: Kuhn-Lakatos-Laudan," *Advances in Child Development and Behavior* 18 (1984): 199.

3. Jean Lipman-Blumen, *Gender Roles and Power* (Englewood Cliffs, N.J.: Prentice-Hall, 1984).

4. See, e.g., Luce Irigaray, *Speculum of the Other Woman*, trans. G. C. Gill (Ithaca, N.Y.: Cornell University Press, 1985); idem, *This Sex Which Is Not One*, trans. C. Porter (Ithaca, N.Y.: Cornell University Press, 1985); E. Fox Keller, *Reflections on Gender and Science* (New Haven: Yale University Press, 1985); Mary Daly, *Beyond God the Father: Toward a Philosophy of Women's Liberation* (Boston: Beacon Press, 1973); idem, *Gyn/ecology: The Metaethics of Radical Feminism* (Boston: Beacon Press, 1978); M. F. Belenky, B. M. Clinchy, N. R. Goldberger, and J. M. Tarule, *Women's Ways of Knowing: The Development of Self, Voice, and Mind* (New York: Basic Books, 1986); Polly Young-Eisendrath, *Hags and Heroes: A Feminist Approach to Jungian Psychotherapy with Couples* (Toronto: Inner City, 1984); idem, "The Female Person and How We Talk About Her," in M. Gergen, ed., *Feminist Thought and the Structure of Knowledge* (New York: New York University Press, 1988); Polly Young-Eisendrath and Florence Wiedemann, *Female Authority: Empowering Women Through Psychotherapy* (New York: Guilford, 1987); and Demaris Wehr, *Jung and Feminism: Liberating Archetypes* (Boston: Beacon Press, 1987), among many others.

5. P. F. Strawson, *Individuals: An Essay in Descriptive Metaphysics* (London: Metheun & Co., 1959); John MacMurray, *Persons in Relation* (New York: Humanities Press, 1954, 1961); and Rom Harre, *Personal Being* (Cambridge: Harvard University Press, 1984). For the quotation cited here, see Harre, *Personal Being*, 26.

6. Ibid., 20.

7. See I. K. Broverman et al., "Sex-role Stereotypes and Clinical Judgments of Mental Health," *Journal of Consulting and Clinical Psychology* 34 (1970): 1–7; and I. K. Broverman et al., "Sex-role Stereotypes: A Current Appraisal," *Journal of Social Issues* 28 (1972): 59–78.

8. Harre, *Personal Being*.

9. E. R. Hall, J. A. Howard, and S. L. Boezio, "Tolerance of Rape: A Sexist or Antisocial Attitude?" *Psychology of Women Quarterly* 10 (1986): 112.

10. S. Gilman, *Difference and Pathology: Stereotypes of Sexuality, Race, and Madness* (Ithaca, N.Y.: Cornell University Press, 1985), 107. Emphasis in original.

11. Kathleen Barry, *Female Sexual Slavery* (New York: New York University Press, 1984), 136.

12. Ibid., 137.

13. See L. E. Walker, *The Battered Woman* (New York: Harper & Row, 1979); and idem, *The Battered Woman Syndrome* (New York: Springer Publishing, 1984).

14. Young-Eisendrath and Wiedemann, *Female Authority*.

15. Walker, *Battered Woman*, 92.

16. Ibid., 93.

17. Barry, *Female Sexual Slavery*, 167.

18. Ibid., 169.

19. Ibid., 67.

20. Ibid., 164.

21. Ibid., 258.

22. Ibid.

23. John Bowlby, "Developmental Psychiatry Comes of Age," unpublished paper, Tavistock Clinic, London, England, 1986.

24. Ibid., 8.

25. W. Ronald Fairbairn, "A Revised Psychopathology of the Psychoses and Psychoneuroses," in W. Ronald Fairbairn, *Psychoanalytic Studies of the Personality* (London: Routledge & Kegan Paul, 1941, 1984).

26. Irigaray, *Speculum of the Other Woman*.

27. Ibid., 181. Emphasis in original.

28. Ibid., 166.

29. Ibid., 167.

30. Harre, *Personal Being*, 105.

31. Carol Turkington, "Sexual Aggression Widespread" *APA Monitor* 18, no. 13 (1987): 15.

32. Ibid.

9

The Transformation
of Suffering:
A Biblical and
Theological Perspective

MARIE F. FORTUNE

A religious person who is victimized by rape, battering, or child sexual abuse frequently faces the questions, Why do I suffer in this way? and, Where is God in my suffering? These profound theological questions cannot be answered simply with platitudes and then dismissed. The question of why there is suffering at all is one of classic theological debate, that is, the question of theodicy, to which there is no completely satisfactory answer. Human suffering in the midst of a world created by a compassionate and loving God is a dimension of human experience which is most disturbing and disquieting. The particular experience of suffering that accompanies victimization by sexual and domestic violence raises particular issues in regard to theodicy.

WHY SUFFERING?

People struggle with two fundamental aspects of the experience of suffering when they ask, Why do I suffer? First is the question of cause, that is, the source of the suffering. The second aspect involves the meaning or purpose of suffering.

Why is there suffering? It suffices to say that some suffering results from arbitrary, accidental sources such as natural disasters. However, much suffering is caused by human sinfulness: sinful acts by some bring suffering to others. These acts can generally be understood as acts of injustice. God allows such sinfulness because God has given persons free will and does not intervene when they choose to engage in

139

unrighteous, unjust acts. Other people suffer from the consequences of these acts. This explanation may be adequate for situations clearly caused by human negligence or meanness, intended or not: for example, a fatal car accident caused by a drunk driver, chronic brown lung disease in textile workers who are denied protection from occupational hazards, birth defects in families living near toxic waste dumps, or incestuous abuse inflicted by a father upon his children. Yet it is still not a wholly satisfactory explanation. Those who suffer search further for answers, or at least for someone to blame.

Victims of sexual or domestic violence have a strong tendency to hold God or themselves responsible for the abuse even though there is clearly a perpetrator whose actions resulted in the victim's suffering. While his/her sinful acts may be understood as a consequence of his/her own brokenness and alienation (sometimes rooted in his/her own victimization), he/she is nonetheless responsible for actions that bring suffering to others. Self-blame or God-blame for one's experience of victimization simply avoids acknowledging that a particular person is responsible for the abusive acts.

Another explanation that is frequently utilized by victims is really old-fashioned superstition. It seeks to explain a current experience of suffering in terms of a previous "sinful" act on the part of the victim: the current suffering is God's punishment for the preceding "sin" which God has judged. Hence a battered woman now being abused by her husband can "explain" why this is happening by remembering that when she was sixteen, she had sexual intercourse once with her boyfriend. She knows this was a "sin" and that God was displeased with her, so God must now be punishing her teenage indiscretion. Or she may have been "disobedient" and not submitted to her husband. She understands the situation to reflect God's acting to bring about her suffering for a justifiable reason; she blames herself and accepts her battering as God's will for her. At least she can "explain" why this happened to her; unfortunately, her explanation leaves no room for questioning her suffering or for confronting her abuser with his responsibility for it.

If God is to blame for the misfortune, one can direct anger at God for causing the suffering. For whatever reason, it is argued, God has singled out the victim of sexual or domestic violence to suffer. Two things result. First she/he is driven away from God by the pain and anger; second, no one is held accountable for what he/she has done to the victims. The suffering of the victim is exacerbated by the feeling that God has sent this affliction to her/him personally and has abandoned her/him in the midst of it. Harold Kushner offers a valuable reframing of this assumption:

> We can maintain our own self-respect and sense of goodness without having to feel that God has judged us and condemned us. We can be angry at what has happened to us, without feeling that we are angry at God. More than that, we can recognize our anger at life's unfairness, our instinctive compassion at seeing people suffer, as coming from God who teaches us to be angry at injustice and to feel compassion for the afflicted. Instead of feeling that we are opposed to God, we can feel that our indignation is God's anger at unfairness working through us, that when we cry out, we are still on God's side, and He [*sic*] is still on ours.[1]

God is not only *not* the cause of injustice and suffering but is instead the source of our righteous anger at the persons or circumstances that do cause suffering as well as our source of compassion for those who suffer.

The second aspect of the experience of suffering involves the attribution of meaning or purpose. What meaning does this experience of suffering hold for the victim? People have great difficulty accepting the irrational and often arbitrary nature of sexual and domestic violence. Instead of realizing that these things happen for no good reason, they attempt to manufacture a good reason or seek a greater good; for example, suffering "builds character" or is "a test of one's faith." The purpose of suffering is then the lesson it teaches, and the result should be a stronger faith in God. Purposefulness somehow softens the pain of the suffering. If some greater good is salvaged, then perhaps the suffering was worth it.

An understanding of the meaning of one's suffering begins with the differentiation between voluntary and involuntary suffering. Voluntary suffering is a painful experience which a person chooses in order to accomplish a greater good. It is optional and is a part of a particular strategy toward a particular end. For example, the acts of civil disobedience by civil rights workers in the United States in the 1960s resulted in police brutality, imprisonment, and sometimes death for these activists. These consequences were unjustifiable but not unexpected. Yet people knowingly chose to endure this suffering in order to change the circumstances of racism, which caused even greater daily suffering for many. Jesus' crucifixion was an act of unjustifiable yet voluntary suffering; in 1 Peter it is viewed as an example:

> For to this you have been called, because Christ also suffered for you, leaving you an example, that you should follow in his steps. He committed no sin; no guile was found on his lips. When he was reviled, he did not revile in return; when he suffered, he did not threaten; but he trusted to [the one] who judges justly. (1 Pet. 2:21–23)

But it is an example not of simply being a sacrificial doormat but of choosing, in the face of the violence of oppressive authority which threatened him, to suffer the consequences of his commitment. It was a witness to his love, not his suffering. Beverly Wildung Harrison further reframes Jesus' suffering on the cross:

> But those who love justice, and have their passion lovingly shaped toward right relation act not because they are enamored of sacrifice. Rather, they are moved by a love strong enough to sustain their action for right relation, even unto death. . . . Jesus' paradigmatic role in the story of our salvation rests not in his willingness to sacrifice himself, but in his passionate love of right relations and his refusal to cease to embody the power-of-relation in the face of that which would thwart it. It was his refusal to desist from radical love, not a preoccupation with sacrifice, which makes his work irreplaceable.[2]

Jesus' crucifixion was the tragic consequence of his faithfulness and refusal to give up his commitment in the face of Roman oppression. He voluntarily accepted the consequence, just as did civil rights workers, in order to bring about a greater good.

Like voluntary suffering, involuntary suffering is unjustifiable under any circumstance. However, unlike voluntary suffering, involuntary suffering is not chosen and never serves a greater good; it is inflicted by a person(s) upon another against their will and results only in pain and destruction. Sexual and domestic violence are forms of involuntary suffering. Neither serves any useful purpose; neither is chosen by the victim; neither is ever justified. Yet both cause great suffering for large numbers of people.

Many victims of involuntary suffering respond with the question: Why did God send *me* this affliction? In the face of the personal crisis of violence, one's deepest need is to somehow explain this experience, to give it specific meaning in one's particular life. By doing this, victims begin to regain some control over the situation and the crisis. If one can point accurately to the cause, perhaps she/he can avoid that circumstance in the future; if one can ascribe meaning, then she/he can give it purpose, can incorporate the experience more quickly and not feel so overwhelmed by it.

Neither superstition nor the search for a greater meaning necessarily encourages the victim of violence to deal with the actual source, that is, the abuser's behavior. Neither encourages the victim to question the abuse she/he is experiencing. Neither motivates the victim to act in seeking justice. Neither is theologically adequate for the person who is struggling to comprehend his/her experience of abuse in light of faith. In Jesus' encounter with the man born blind (John 9:1–12), he is confronted with the question about the cause of suffering.[3] "And his disciples asked him, 'Rabbi, who sinned, this man or his parents, that he was born blind?' " (v. 2). Jesus answers their question in terms of the meaning rather than the cause of his suffering: "It was not that this man sinned, or his parents, but that the works of God might be made manifest in him. We must work the works of [the one] who sent me while it is day; night comes, when no one can work" (vv. 3–4).

Jesus proceeds to make a medicine and heal the man's blindness. He dismisses the request for a superstitious cause and restates the search for meaning. The blind man's suffering is a fact. Where is God in this suffering; what can God do in this situation; and what are we called to do? Jesus acts to relieve suffering rather than discuss its cause. He is teaching that the responsibility belongs to us to act regardless.[4] The question for us is not who sinned (in cosmic terms) or how can God allow women to be beaten and raped, but how can *we* allow this to go unchallenged? In challenging this victimization, the question is, Who is accountable for this suffering and how can justice be wrought here?

What Jesus does not address in this parable is the situation in which there is clear responsibility for the suffering of another. A more current reading of this story might include the information that the man's father beat his mother during her pregnancy with him, and the child's blindness resulted. In this case, when asked the question who sinned, Jesus might have said, "The one who beat his mother is accountable for his acts. Rebuke him. If he repents, forgive him. [See Luke 17:1–4.] Here we must work the works of the one who sent me." Part of that work, which is clearly expected in the prophetic tradition of Hebrew and Christian theology, is that of calling to repentance and accountability and making justice in order to accomplish forgiveness, healing, and reconciliation. These responses to experiences of suffering at the hands of another are requisite if the suffering is to be more than simply endured.

ENDURANCE

In both the explanation of superstition and the attribution of greater meaning, God is held responsible for the suffering itself. This presupposes a belief in God as omnipotent and omniscient. If God is in control and choosing to exercise that control by bringing suffering upon the afflicted as punishment or in order to teach them something, then both cause and meaning are clearly determined to be in God's hands.

In the face of this interpretive framework, most victims accept endurance as the means of dealing with this suffering. Deciding that being battered or molested is justifiable punishment, one's lot in life, cross to bear, or God's will, sets in motion a pattern of endurance that accepts victimization and seeks ways to coexist with it. Victims are encouraged to endure when support and advocacy to get away from the violence are not provided, when they are told to go home and keep praying, and when they are expected to keep the family together even though the violence continues and they are in danger. This "doormat theology" teaches that it is God's will that people suffer and the only option is to endure it. There is no space to question or challenge the suffering that comes from this injustice, to feel anger, or to act to change one's circumstance. The result of this theology is that a victim remains powerless and victimized and her/his physical, psychological, and spiritual survival are jeopardized. This understanding of the meaning of suffering comforts the comfortable and afflicts the afflicted but ignores the demands of a God who seeks justice and promises abundance of life.

There is no virtue in enduring suffering if no greater good is at stake. Certainly, being battered or sexually abused is such a situation. There is *no greater good* for anyone—certainly not for the victim and children and others who witness the violence but also not for the abuser. Endurance that merely accepts the violence ignores the abuser's sinfulness and denies him a chance for repentance and redemption which may come from holding him accountable for his acts. Endurance in order to "keep the family together" is a sham because the family is already broken apart by the abuse. There is no virtue to be gained in this situation where everyone loses; there is no virtue in encouraging a victim of abuse to accept and endure it.

TRANSFORMATION

For the Christian, the theology of the cross and the resurrection provides insight into the meaning of suffering and transformation. God did not send Jesus to the cross as a test of his faith, as punishment for his sin, or to build his character. The Romans crucified Jesus and made him a victim of overt and deadly anti-Semitic violence. It was a devastating experience for Jesus' followers who watched him murdered. They were overwhelmed by fear, despair, and meaninglessness. They left the scene of the crucifixion feeling abandoned and betrayed by God. The resurrection and subsequent events were the surprising realization that in the midst of profound suffering, God is present and new life is possible.

This retrospective realization in no way justified the suffering: it transformed it. It presented the possibility of new life coming forth from the pain of suffering. Sometimes Jesus' crucifixion is misinterpreted as being the model for suffering: since Jesus went to the cross, persons should bear their own crosses of irrational violence (for example, rape) without complaint. But Jesus' crucifixion does not sanctify suffering. It remains a witness to the horror of violence done to another and an identification with the suffering that people experience. It is not a model of how suffering should be borne but a witness to God's desire that no one should have to suffer such violence again. The resurrection, the realization that the Christ was present to the disciples and is present to us, transformed but never justified the suffering and death experience. The people were set free from the pain of that experience to realize the newness of life among them in spite of suffering.

Personal violence presents a victim with two options: endurance and acceptance of continued suffering, or an occasion for transformation. Endurance means remaining a victim; transformation means becoming a survivor.

In order to become a survivor and transform one's suffering, persons must use their strength and all available resources within themselves and from others to move away from a situation in which violence continues unabated. God is present in this movement as a means to transformation. A young woman, raped at age eighteen, reflected on

145

her rape experience in light of her faith. As she recovered, she observed that her prayer life had shifted dramatically after the assault. Prior to the rape, she recalled that her prayers most often took the form of "Dear God, please take care of me." As she recovered from the rape, she realized that now her prayers began, "Dear God, please help me to remember what I have learned." She moved from a passive, powerless position of victim in which she expected God to protect her to a more mature and confident position of survivor in which she recognized her own strength and responsibility to care for herself with God's help. In addition, her compassion and empathy for others increased and she was empowered to act to change things that cause violence and suffering. She was able to transform her experience and mature in her faith as she recovered from the assault with the support of family and friends.

One of the most profound fears experienced by one who suffers is that God is literally abandoning her/him. The experience of suffering and the resulting righteous anger in the face of that suffering need not separate us from God. Paul gives witness to this in Romans.

> For I am sure that neither death, nor life, nor angels, nor principalities, nor things present, nor things to come, nor powers, nor height, nor depth, nor anything else in all creation, will be able to separate us from the love of God in Christ Jesus our Lord. (Rom. 8:38)

God is not responsible for suffering; God is not pleased by people's suffering; God suffers with us and is present to us in the midst of the pain of sexual and domestic violence; God does not abandon us even though everyone else may. This is the promise of the Hebrew and Christian texts—that God is present in the midst of suffering and that God gives us the strength and courage to resist injustice and to transform suffering.

Just as God does not will people to suffer, God does not send suffering in order that people have an occasion for transformation. It is a fact of life that people do suffer. The real question is not, Why? but, What do people do with that suffering? Transformation is the alternative to endurance and passivity. It is grounded in the conviction of hope and empowered by a passion for justice in the face of injustice. It is the faith that the way things are is not the way things have to be. It is a trust in righteous anger in the face of evil which pushes people to action. Transformation is the means by which, refusing to accept injustice and refusing to assist its victims to endure suffering any longer, people act. We celebrate small victories, we chip away at oppressive attitudes cast in concrete, we say no in unexpected places, we speak boldly of things deemed secret and unmentionable, we stand with those who are trapped in victimization to support their journeys to safety and healing, and we break the cycle of violence we may have known in our own lives. By refusing to endure evil and by seeking to transform suffering, we are about God's work of making justice and healing brokenness.

NOTES

1. Harold S. Kushner, *When Bad Things Happen to Good People* (New York: Schocken Books, 1981), 45.

2. Beverly Wildung Harrison, *Making the Connections* (Boston: Beacon Press, 1985), 18–19.

3. "It is assumed that sin, by whomsoever committed, was the cause of the blindness. This was the common belief in Judaism; see e.g. *Shabbath* 55a: There is no death without sin (proved by Ezek. 18:20) and no punishment (i.e., sufferings) without guilt (proved by Ps. 89:33). When a man has been blind from birth, the sin must be sought either in the man's parents, or in his own ante-natal existence" (C. K. Barrett, *The Gospel According to St. John* [London: SPCK, 1955], 294).

4. In light of the Holocaust some have asked, Where was God? and many Jews have reframed the question to, Where were the people who could have stopped this?

10

Pain and Pleasure: Avoiding the Confusions of Christian Tradition in Feminist Theory

BEVERLY W. HARRISON / CARTER HEYWARD

As political repression accelerates in the United States, feminists must sharpen their critiques of the cultural, social, religious, and economic roots of women's oppression. It is imperative, moreover, that in this reactionary climate feminist theorists admit the complexity of the reconstructive perspectives they are attempting to forge. Theories that oversimplify the constructive feminist agenda or challenge the troubling dualisms of patriarchal culture in an overly reactive way merely feed the divisiveness among women that political repression seeks to sow.

Contemporary feminist politics and theory, liberal and radical, converge in the face of pervasive violence against women and mounting efforts to foreclose the already limited options that women have regarding reproductive choice and health care. But in discussions about pornography, or about what constitutes an optimal conception of women's eroticism, consensus among feminists gives way to acrimony, and our politics tend to become a battleground of conflicting normative theories and strategies.[1] In matters of sex, more than in any other political arena, feminists are inclined simply to superimpose their individual preferences or senses of morality upon others. In this way, the feminist insistence that "the personal is political" (and, conversely, that the political always yields personal, concrete meaning) ironically receives skewed, negative confirmation rather than constructive expression. That the personal is political is a social fact, and our personal preferences and sensibilities always are steeped in a more complex

148

social dialectic. These personal preferences acquire moral meaning in relation to the well-being of a larger social-cultural order. As it is, among contemporary feminists, wherever eros, sex, and sexuality are envisioned differently, conflicting personal agendas jockey competitively to become the "right" answer to the public question of which strategies and policies actually contribute to the liberation of women.

While we agree with Marianne Valverde that "the debate on sexuality has not been one of the success stories of the women's movement,"[2] we also acknowledge the oft-repeated claim that, from a historical point of view, the greatest breakthrough of contemporary feminist theory is precisely this securing of the cultural and intellectual space to forge a genuine female "discourse on sexuality."[3] Conflict over sexuality should not obscure this gain. The burgeoning feminist literature on sexuality, including discussions of pornography and sadomasochistic practice among women, has brought sex out of the closet into the realm of public discourse and has sharpened reflection among feminists on their values. On all sides of these contemporary debates, feminists agree that relational dynamics of domination and submission, images and acts that ritualize violence, make widespread contributions to the sexual pleasure of men—and women—in our society.[4] In other words, it is beyond dispute that many women find sexual pleasure in patterns of erotic domination and submission, whether these images lurk largely in the realm of women's sexual fantasies or are acted out in women's sex lives.

We are grateful for the work of the many secular feminists who have been unwilling to let specific questions of eros and sex go unexplored, a failing, as we see it, of many religious feminists. This essay is an attempt by two religious feminists to integrate and expand insights from this discussion of women's eroticism and genital pleasure. We share with many secular feminists a conviction that feminist theory must incorporate a profound positive evaluation of the vitality of the erotic in women's lives. We understand eros to be body-centered energy channeled through longing and desire. With Audre Lorde we affirm eroticism as essential to our well-being and believe it to be the source of creative personal power and, as such, essential to creativity.[5] In our work, we have attempted to show how eros also is central to an adequate feminist theory not only of politics but of religious and moral experience.[6] We also share the suspicion, now widely voiced in feminist literature, that resistance to pervasive pornographic manipulation is tempting some feminists to embrace a subtle prudery or a new anti-sexual moralism.[7] That women now must seek sexual fulfillment in a context where "pleasure and danger"[8] are intertwined seems to us obvious. The threat of violence and the objectification of women's bodies create genuine barriers to women's realization of the erotic, but the way forward is not to adopt prematurely a feminist theory of women's sexuality that portrays women's sexual needs simplistically, as if our desires were homogeneous or untouched by the disordered power dynamics of patriarchal eroticism.

Feminist theorists whose insights contribute most to the emerging discourse on sexuality are those who have been most attentive to the sociohistorical shifts in patterns of eroticism, recognizing that forms of sexual expression and erotic desire, while rooted in physio-psychic potential, are shaped by complex cultural dynamics—recognizing, that is, that sexuality and eroticism have a history. This history of sexuality is embedded in social structures of patterned power relations such as institutionalized heterosexism, racism, and cultural imperialism.[9] To explore how senses of personal power and eroticism have been linked historically in heterosexist patriarchy is to begin also to see that the self/other relation which elicits strong erotic desire frequently is one of domination and submission. As such, sex is often experienced as a dynamic of conquest and surrender rather than as power in mutual relation.[10]

In such "eroticization of domination," sexual desire is linked with either self-oblivion or self-assertion. It would be ahistorical and naive to imagine that *anyone's* eroticism in this culture could be untouched by this dynamic.[11] Feminists such as Valverde and Linda Gordon insist that the "eroticization of equality" must be understood as a historical project of feminism. They acknowledge, however, that this project is necessarily long term,[12] so securely fastened in our society, and our psyches, is the felt need for a sexual mediation of relational power to confirm our superiority or subjection in relation to others, whether for a moment or a lifetime.

To probe the linkage of erotic desire and inequality so characteristic of patriarchal culture we need to focus on the subtle connection between relational dynamics of domination and submission and erotic experiences of pain and pleasure. We realize that this connection—between experiences of relational power or powerlessness and of sexual pleasure enhanced by pain—might be approached critically from a number of directions (e.g., natural or social science; art, literature, or film; comparative studies of religion or culture), as well as with different focuses (e.g., gender relations, sexual customs, ascetic traditions). As feminist ethicists and theologians who are Christian, we approach this issue with a critical interest in the role of Christianity in developing and sustaining a social (not only sexual) relation—a sadomasochistic relation—in which pleasure is available chiefly through pain. We are committed, moreover, to participation in the reconstruction of theological and moral theory which is both socially responsible, contributing to the creation of justice for all, and deeply affirmative of erotic pleasure as a source of moral good.

We will now examine some Christian theological roots of the equation of pain with pleasure and also suggest ways in which the legacy of liberal individualism, the dominant ideological underpinning of Western society, tempts feminists to reformulate the dilemmas of female eroticism in a way that perpetuates rather than challenges this theologically legitimated confusion. We shall conclude with images showing how erotic relationships might contribute to fully socialized, self-and-other-empowering relations.

PAIN AS PLEASURE: CHRISTIAN FOUNDATIONS

Christian orthodoxy (culminating for the Western church in Augustine) eschewed the notion of a radical dualism in which Creator and Creation exist in a posture of *unmitigated* opposition. Orthodox Christian dualism, by comparison to more radically dualistic religious systems eventually deemed heretical, has been more experientially complex, more dialectical in the relation between cosmologically "higher" and "lower" realities.[13]

Still, the primary architect of the identification of pain with pleasure in Western culture has been the Christian church with its basically dualistic anthropology. On the basis of Neoplatonic cosmology, early church fathers explained their religious experience as essentially that of breaking tension between such oppositional realities as spirit and flesh, male and female, light and dark, good and evil.[14] The role of religion in general, Christian religion in particular, was thus to mitigate the opposition by enabling the two forces to "co-operate" rather than to compete for the headship of society as well as the human soul. Such opposites as spirit and flesh, male and female, could be cooperative only insofar as the higher was in control of the lower—and as the lower accepted its place as a weaker reality, both naturally and morally subordinate in relation to the higher. Whether by will or force, the resolution of tension between potentially competitive cosmic forces was to become a test of Christian faith: a faithful Christian woman, for example, would accept her role gladly as man's helper and a faithful Christian man would accept his role cheerfully as head of the household. Patristic theological discourse bears written testimony to social relations of domination and subjugation in which "the fathers" of the family (both civil and ecclesial households)[15] believed that they should be in charge of women, children, slaves, and all other creatures—and in control, moreover, of their own "lower" selves: flesh, body, passions, and eroticism.

Because in this system good Christian men—and through men's authority, women as well—must deny the enjoyment of flesh, females, darkness, evil, and the sensuality associated with these negativities, early Christian anthropology required that *pain*—the *deprivation of sensual pleasure*—be accepted as an important element in attaining the joy of salvation. We cannot trace here the long process by which this dualistic asceticism in which the exercise of faith involved attempts to transcend the sensual pleasures of human being—hunger for food, warmth, and touch—became in time not only acceptable as a dimension of Christian spirituality, but moreover normative for it: to be Christian was to accept or even to seek pain.

This establishment of antisensual pain as a foundation of Christian faith is a complex story informed by diverse historical processes. For example, the extended sociopolitical repression, torture, and martyrdom that some Christians endured and that threatened others in the Roman Empire in the middle of the third and during the early fourth centuries contributed to the spiritualizing of deprivation and suffering. But it is one thing to accept suffering for the sake of a moral or religious good when confronting unjust power, and another to perceive suffering as itself an intrinsic moral or religious value, the point to which much institutional Christianity came after the collapse of the Roman Imperium.

The earlier anti-material, anti-body, anti-woman dualisms of Neoplatonic patriarchal Christianity laid the groundwork for this romanticization of suffering but the full flowering of masochism in the Christian ethic can be best measured by the increase, over time, of a sex-phobic and sex-preoccupied focus within the Christian ethic.[16] Historian Samuel Laeuchli has traced one strand of the story of this move from a Christian spiritual discipline focused at least in part on resistance to the Roman state to one morbidly preoccupied with the control of human sexuality.[17] Laeuchli acknowledges that this development had deep roots in early dualistic patristic theory about spirit and flesh and in the developing church's transparent fear of women.[18] Not insignificantly for feminist theory, Laeuchli also connects this impulse to sexual control and the rapid development of centralized ecclesiastical hierarchy within Western Christianity. We can only speculate as to how such dynamics of pain and pleasure took hold of Christian experience such that the suffering associated with sensual self-denial became *essential* to Christian spiritual and moral life, and thereby a source of spiritual satisfaction. Without pain, pleasure was immoral; whereas by pain, with pain, and through pain, pleasure became a happy consequence of the Christian pilgrimage.

This spiritual paradigm of Christian pain as virtue and as pleasure was also developed theologically: The Christian drama of salvation has been staged historically as a transaction between an almighty God and a powerless humanity. As the lower relational entity, humanity has been cast as a "fallen" partner, able to be "saved" or "redeemed" into right relation only insofar as human beings know ourselves to be unworthy of anything but punishment from God. Into our unworthy lives comes Jesus, the Christ, to bear our sins and to submit, on our behalf, to the Father God's Will. Thus, standing in for us (as only the elder obedient Son is worthy to do in this patriarchal schema), Jesus is humiliated and killed, becoming thereby a perfect sacrifice to the Father. As the classical portrait of the punitive character of this divine-human transaction, Anselm of Canterbury's doctrine of the atonement (1093–1109) probably represents the sadomasochism of Christian teaching at its most transparent.

But there is a subtler sadomasochistic hue to Christianity, an effect also of the litany of dualistic oppositions such as those between earth and heaven, flesh and spirit, and present and future. The patriarchal Christian story is basically one of a fierce war between good and evil forces in the cosmos, from the farthest outreaches of the universe to the individual's soul. In this praxis of opposition, Christians have believed that, in fact, God—the supreme force for good—already has won the war. This faith has reflected the Christian experience on two different levels of meaning in their lives: God's victory is on a spiritual level whereas the numerous incessant battles which constitute the war are material as well. Christians have believed that the spiritual power of the resurrection has overcome human history and thus the pain of the cross, so real in "this world," has been vanquished by the power of God in the "other world" above or beyond us. We may catch glimpses even now of the spiritual world through faith that embodied life as we know it is not all there is.

But for most people on the earth embodied *pain* is much of all there is—the pain of poverty, oppression, alienation, loss and, from a liberation perspective, the pain incurred in struggling against injustice and oppression. In Christian theology, eternal joy may have the upper hand and the spiritual victory, but daily pain and sorrow play the more visceral, sensual roles in shaping the lives of most women, men, and children on earth. This split sensibility between what is experienced and what is yearned for provides, for many Christians, a foundation for their faith. This faith in turn functions as a state of mind, a cosmology, and as a way of interpreting daily events and historical movement.

In this dualistic praxis that is not peculiar to Christianity, yet which takes a distinctive shape in Christian theology, *pain* in the present and *hope* for the future together form a bridge between earth and heaven, human and divine life, estrangement and unity, conflict and resolution. Pain and hope thereby constitute the link for most Christians between such immediate sensual experiences as hunger and loneliness and such "delayed gratification" as food and intimacy. This tension, existential and political, personal and historical, provides an eschatological backdrop against which sadomasochism is acted out as the most typically "Christian" of all social relations: We learn to experience the deprivation of pleasure—the pain of being hurt, hungry, or rejected; of feeling weak, stupid, bad in the immediate present—as a moment filled with intense anticipation of pleasure that is yet to come. In short, Christians learn theologically to equate the anticipation of pleasure with pleasure itself. This disembodied sensibility, in which *pleasure is fundamentally a state of mind,* is steeped in the eschatological promise that the realm of the divine—a spiritual arena of unity, joy and ecstasy—is, for Christians, here but not quite here; now but not quite yet.

The covert popularity among Christians of pain-filled sexual (and other social) relations can be explained in part by this politic of pain and hope that is so basic to classical Christian practice and theory and that is as forceful and erotic a politic in the lives of women as of men. This difficult social relation is rooted most deeply, we submit, in the pain of alienation generated historically by political and religious structures of domination and control. Such structures as male gender superiority and white racial supremacy have shaped to an extent the relational dynamics and erotic feelings of all members of all institutions and societies that are themselves established on these foundations of domination and control. Thus do *all* Christians, as well as many others, bear scars of sadomasochistic relations.

Beyond a common experience as dreamers of an eschatological relief and pleasure, Christian men and women have a very different political and sexual history, a point that, thanks to feminist religious scholarship, is finally widely acknowledged today.[19] The differences between them are nowhere more apparent than in the ways in which Christian sadomasochism is actually embodied by the sons of the Father, on the one hand, and his daughters on the other.

Consider the sons: Unless reconstructed along the lines of a feminist liberation hermeneutic, or of a radical womanism, Christianity—even in its most liberal dress—remains quintessentially a religion about men controlling men's bodies, men's women, men's children, and men's other property. This fundamental male-male relation is imaged as that between father and son. The father is willful and benevolent, loving and just, one who desires—but does not always receive—obedience from his sons, in which case the sons can be punished justly. (Apologists for the sexism of Christianity are apt to insist that the "sons" include the "daughters." To the extent that the daughters fall for such patriarchal "inclusion," we can read ourselves into this drama of disobedience and discipline.)

The explicit sadomasochistic dynamics of classical Christianity do not often receive voice in "modern" Christian theologies. Even so, they live on in the sexual fantasies of many Christian men and are frequently expressed in closeted homosexual eroticism so much denied and so widely practiced among Christian males. This is especially true among those men drawn to traditional Catholic liturgical spirituality—perhaps because this spirituality offers such dramatic opportunity to dress up, role play, and act out a very sensual relation between men. In a much more literal way than at the altar, the "meat-rack" is often the arena for enacting the justice of the father who must whip his sons, humiliate them, and require them to beg for his mercy. The sons' pain is merely in proportion to what they deserve for the sin of their disobedience which, in the dualistic praxis we have described above, *includes their experiences of sexual passion.* The sadistic father will feel pleasure in disciplining his sons "for their own good." Masochistic sons will enjoy the discipline because it will set them into right relation with their father, whose love they seek.

But did not Jesus suffer and die in their stead? Why is there this violence between father and son if the ransom for the wages of sin has been exacted already? Perhaps it is the guilt of the younger sons in relation to the innocent Jesus? Or their catholic desire for participation? Or simply their need for hands-on experience? Most of these sons believe that with Jesus they too must be beaten and broken in order to satisfy their almighty father. Becoming Christ-like—good sons, submissive to the father's will—is accomplished repeatedly and ritualistically through a pain which the sons experience as the love of God and as such a source of deep satisfaction and pleasure. In this erotic fantasy, the father is turned on by his absolute power over another.

A theology of scourged buttocks and torn anuses, and the accompanying violence, can nevertheless be understood as a yearning, a reaction, of Christian men *against* the dualistic character of the divine-human relation in which no son except Jesus has immediate access to the Father; nor for that matter does the Father have intimate relations with his human sons. The sadomasochistic sexual relation between Christian "fathers" and "sons" might be comprehended as a father-son transaction in which is expressed their mutual desire for immediate and intimate relation.[20]

To be sure, not all Christian men are driven to enact this sadomasochistic imaging of divine-human relations. But we believe that Christianity has intensely eroticized male-male transactions of subordination and dominance, obedience and defiance. In the face of this we interpret much male fear of sexuality as a defense against these desires and interpret the lure of celibacy within Christianity as a fragile defense against them.

Since the Protestant Reformation, which reestablished "compulsory heterosexuality," male sexual transactions with women have frequently been interpreted as "duty"—a "burden" to be assumed by spiritual and intellectual superiors toward inferiors. We perceive the continuing split in male eroticism, in which sex and intimacy are rarely associated,

156

as historically conditioned by these dynamics of gender inequality. Men who are "turned on" to women are rarely turned on by strong, self-reliant women or women who make demands for full integrated relationship. The objectification of women as "sex objects" is sustained primarily by the split in men's lives—between sex and intimacy, friendship and eroticism, man and man, and man's sense of "spirit" and his own body. "Woman" has become historically a convenient scapegoat for men's lack of sexual and spiritual integration.[21]

Consider now the daughters of God. However harshly men may be dealt with by God in the sadomasochistic imagination, the raison d'être behind the discipline they receive is to make them worthy to share in the father's inheritance, his power and dominion over his kingdom. Patriarchal daughters by contrast are not heirs at all but rather are their brothers' helpers on the way toward men's appropriation of the power of God. As the sons are redeemed by their obedience to God, so too are the daughters redeemed by their obedience to the sons.

Patriarchal heterosexism is founded less upon deep male heterosexual desire than upon men's use of women's bodies as a means of public social control. In this situation, women have no body rights, no moral claim to our bodies as self-possessed. In Christianity, woman is equated with flesh, body, but Christian women have no integrity of embodied selfhood; no authoritative voice in determining where we put our bodies/ourselves, with whom we share our bodies/ourselves, where we put our embodied energies, time, and talents. *Women in Christianity are meant to live for others.* The inability of so many women even to imagine that they should be well-treated in a relationship with a man or that they deserve physical and emotional pleasure is conditioned by the demand that we have our being for others.

Women's bodies, sensual and hungry, are on the one hand needy impediments to the sacrifices expected of us. On the other hand, our bodies are all we have, all we are, and as such are our best and only hope. If Christian women are to be liberated, it will be through the aegis of our sensual, hungry, needy bodyselves, which we learn are dangerous, dirty, and bad—and, at the same time, the source of our power. Such body alienation is then reinforced by the pervasive threat of rape, sexual harassment, and other widespread forms of bodily exploitation. Thus do we learn to live in radical ambivalence toward our bodies/ourselves. The very womanly flesh we learn to despise is the source of our redemption—from material and spiritual bondage, from self-loathing and from our contempt for women in general. As feminists attempt to show, the possibility of women's liberation is seeded in women's self-respect, a revolutionary act because it embodies a challenge to fundamental assumptions about womanhood which have been espoused both by the church and by Western societies for two milleniums.

While feminists speak often with passion and good reason about women's self-respect, being woman-identified, taking women seriously, we should not underestimate the force—and devastating effects—of misogyny in patriarchal heterosexist Christianity and in those cultures shaped largely by it. It is far easier to embrace feminist ideology in our public work than to live radically in a strong love for our bodies/ourselves, or with love and advocacy for our sisters.

While we acknowledge the sexual sadomasochism acted out among Christian women as well as men, we believe that sexual sadomasochism is, as we have suggested, a sexual politic of male-male relations—even when the participants include females. All women in patriarchy are, to a degree, male-identified. To that extent, we are likely to enjoy sado-masochistic relations, sexual and other.[22] The shape of sadomasochism among women, however, is probably less genitally sexual than among men. More often, female sadomasochism is more generally sensual, more a matter of women's body-integrity.[23] For this reason a more clearly female embodiment of sadomasochism originates not in our desire to control others but in an ambivalence toward our bodies. This is reflected in bodily obsessions such as fear of aging, fixation on cosmetic beauty, and eating disorders which have grown to epidemic proportions in our time and culture.[24]

Eating disorders provide an especially poignant illustration of sado-masochism among women because they embody, literally and vividly, the confusion of pain and pleasure. Whether an eating disorder takes the form of anorexia nervosa (self-starvation), bulimia (gorging oneself with food and then purging oneself of it), or compulsive overeating, its source is pain—social, political, and emotional pain—and its consequences are a short-lived pleasure which becomes pain and which continues the cycle of self-destructive behavior. The eating disorder signals a woman's resistance to the role imposed upon her body/herself by her religion or culture.[25] It represents, moreover, a woman's ambivalence toward her body/herself. An anorexic woman, for example, wants to be thin since thinness is a virtue, and a pleasure, in men's eyes (and, thereby, her own). She is willing to starve herself, literally to death if need be, to become thin enough to enjoy herself. Another woman, who is bulimic, takes pleasure in eating—and wants to be thin. She experiences tension between pleasing herself with food and pleasing men (and, thereby, herself) with a trim figure. This tension generates a pattern of compulsive eating finally more painful than pleasurable, to be followed by compulsive elimination of the food. For the bulimic the pleasure of eating has become painful, and the pain of induced vomiting becomes a relief and a pleasure. Rather than make public challenge to institutions that teach misogyny, or embody this protest in her work and relationships (perhaps more common today), the woman internalizes the misogyny and punishes herself for daring to dream of her own liberation. From a psychoanalytic perspective, the daughter has internalized the father and, as such, acts sadistically toward herself—and toward her mother. The heart of the problem, the woman's masochism, far from being "natural," is the psychosocial result of the patriarchal aim to help women accept, even enjoy, our powerlessness in relation to men and the pain we necessarily will incur if we attempt to alter this relation.

The dynamics of Christian heterosexist sadomasochism, sketched only in bold relief here, are no longer *explicitly* emphasized in the theologies of liberal Christianity, that is, in those Christian communities that do not contend against the modern scientific world view. Here Christian asceticism has given way to a qualified embrace of the value of the created world. The blatant antisensuality bias of the highest forms of patristic and medieval spirituality has been replaced by the more dialectical dualism characteristic of the early church. Liberal Christians affirm embodied sensuality when it is expressed in heterosexual monogamous marriage, perceiving that interpersonal intimacy and love redeem sex; they have transmitted eros to a spiritual plane.[26] Christian women, in particular, learn an erotic patterning in which eros is affirmed if and when it is expressed in "love" relations with men. The modern female disposition to "fall madly in love," to be "swept away" in order to justify sexual desire, surely has its roots in this liberal shift.[27]

In our view, the Christian theological liberal response to the need for a more adequate theory of eros is unsatisfactory. Some theological liberalism, for instance, rejects sadomasochistic imagery of divine mediation by qualifying or repudiating the Anselmnian doctrine of atonement.[28] While stressing the ethical character of divine and human interaction, this theological posture nonetheless maintains a bias toward the spiritual, thereby perpetuating a subtle devaluation of both material and female existence.[29] Here the doctrine of the inferiority of women is replaced by a complementarity doctrine in which women (good women, those who express their sexuality in lifelong committed heterosexual relations) are in fact more spiritual, less carnal, than men. This teaching, which continues to tempt Christian feminism and postchristian theory to adopt a dualistic doctrine of female erotic supremacy in which women are more spiritual than men, serves to reduce the pressure for a theological reconstruction of the terms of divine-human interaction predicated by Christian patriarchal imagination. It also frequently leads Christian or formerly Christian feminist theorists to evade the full religious and ethical impact of the secular feminist struggle to place women's sexuality at the heart of a feminist liberation theory.

FEMINIST RESPONSE TO PATRIARCHAL CHRISTIAN MASOCHISM

Even so, most postchristian and Christian liberation feminists have positioned themselves in opposition to the basic masochistic assumptions about women's spirituality generated by orthodox patriarchal Christianity. Insofar as religious feminists acknowledge embodied pleasure as fundamentally life-enhancing, we join many secular feminist theorists and, with them, affirm a post-Enlightenment, modern stance against the antisexual obsession of Christian metaphysics. In our view, a dramatic recovery of a world-affirming, sex-affirming perspective could not have occurred without the rupture that post-Enlightenment modernity created between dominant Christian ecclesiastical culture and a secular, world- and human-experience-centered way of interpreting the world. Though many interpreters have recognized that the basic cultural shift stemming from the Enlightenment led to a recovery of this-worldly interest, few have observed the fact that the shift characteristic of this transition is one in which concrete, worldly pleasure is positively embraced. In some post-Enlightenment theory it is even predicated as "the highest good."[30] One need not endorse a full-scale hedonistic psychology or the monistic value theory that it entails in order to acknowledge the critical character of this shift for human well-being.

The long struggle required to recover a respectful appreciation of the centrality of pleasure to human fulfillment and the essential role of eros and sex in human well-being would never have occurred if the political and theological control exercised by patriarchal Christianity had not been displaced. Yet we submit that it is one thing to break the ecclesiastical monopoly on the definition of the relation of spiritual pleasure and physical pain, and another to disentangle, at the level of personal erotic experience, a clear difference between what hurts and what gives pleasure. Physiologically, the line between pain and pleasure is at times a fine one. It is not surprising that human beings learn a psychological preference for an eroticism that is tinged, if not with pain, with tension that is close to pain. We suspect, however, that the widespread cultural entanglement of violence and sex reflects a blurred distinction between pain and pleasure in many people's experience, and moreover that few people experience tension-free relationships as erotic.

It is the clear intent of most feminist theorists to affirm pleasure and the importance of seeking its enhancement as a path to deeper personal power. Were the modern post-Enlightenment embrace of the erotic its only legacy, feminist reconstruction could proceed with an agenda of affirming women's eroticism without contradiction. But Enlightenment tradition, with its gradual affirmation of embodiment, nevertheless maintained a strong continuity with Christian patriarchal interpretation of the meaning of *personal power in relationship*. In fact, modern liberal theory, with its uncritical commitment to capitalism, exacerbated the patriarchal imaging of self-other relations as nonmutual. The individualism of the Enlightenment became, increasingly, a conception of social relations in which power-in-relation, if not antagonistic, is at least competitive such that either self *or* other must prevail. In this schema, personal power and personal fulfillment are envisaged as the realization of "autonomy," understood as "self-possession" or as *freedom from dependency*.[31]

The basic philosophical and political tenets of so-called free societies are suffused with such assumptions. Feminists too have been schooled by life as well as books in a highly individualized and possessive understanding of personal power: an ability to generate action, a capacity to effect. Our power, we see clearly, includes our feelings which can serve to catapult us into commitment or action. We must not forget that in the West (especially in the United States), our senses of personal power (including our feelings), our sexualities (how we use this power), and our eroticism (our specifically *sexual* feelings) *always* are mediated to a degree by these deities of individualism and possession. A feminist reconstruction of sexual theory must acknowledge that the continuing confusion between pain and pleasure that besets patriarchal Christianity cannot be disentangled without also challenging the bias that personal pleasure consists primarily in the realization of independence. Both patriarchal Christianity's hierarchical social relations, characterized by domination and submission (however benignly exercised), *and* a feminist commitment to a woman's self-possession (rather than her being possessed by others) continue to reflect a dualistic apprehension of embodied power and thus an erotic split.

The effect of the split between top and bottom and between male and female (patriarchal distinctions), and between belonging to oneself and belonging to others (a liberal dichotomy sustained in much feminism) is to associate the erotic with ongoing tension. Patriarchy has conditioned us to feel, as erotic, the tension between top and bottom, male and female, self and other. While most feminists have rejected flatly the hierarchical- and gender-based dualisms, individual feminists often remain captive to the need for relational tension.[32] Even some of the most subtle feminist theory has not yet adequately repudiated the association of eroticism with the split between self and other that is endemic to the patriarchal view of reality. In other words, if we are likely to be "turned on" in patriarchal praxis by being on top or on bottom, giver or receiver, in traditional male or female roles, we may still, in feminist praxis, be "turned on" by a sense of being *either* self-possessed *or* belonging to another. In the context of this dualistic eroticism, *for a woman to feel that she belongs both to herself and to another is rare*. To do so involves breaking the tension generated by the split between oneself and others. To those shaped by the power relations of patriarchal culture (all of us), the loss of such tension is experienced unavoidably as the diminishment or elimination of erotic power. Few are able to find their way, in this dualistic praxis, to full eroticization in mutuality.[33]

This may suggest why so many people (feminists and others) find it hard to sustain high levels of sexual excitement in the context of friendship.[34] It suggests also that the erotic split is the ground upon which we learn to feel as pleasurable or sexually stimulating that which in fact is the source of much pain to us: our alienation from one another, as people who have difficulty *feeling* power by *sharing* it. To put it another way, it is rare in this culture to experience power when shared as *genuine power* because we are inured to perceiving as powerful anything that does not have a zero-sum quantity, that does not appear "over against" us or someone else. As we have already insisted, the identification of eros with the tension created by power disparity cannot be transcended until we repudiate the legacies of patriarchal social relations at root, rejecting the way patriarchy images self-other relationship.

An illustration of how feminist theorists miss the mark here can be illustrated by examining an interesting and theoretically suggestive article by Jessica Benjamin entitled "Master and Slave."[35] Benjamin seeks to illuminate "the violence of erotic domination," particularly as it is evidenced in heterosexual relations. She has been criticized by a lesbian-feminist defender of sadomasochistic sex, Gayle Rubin—unfairly, in our judgment—for seeking to find "a middle ground" between the new feminist sexual prudery and libertinism.[36] Unlike Rubin, we take at face value Benjamin's insistence that what she seeks is an understanding of the *appeal* of ritualized sadomasochistic sexual practice rather than a simplistic condemnation of it. She does not place herself outside the cultural dynamics she is analyzing. She recognizes that in ritualizing sadomasochistic sex practice, such violence is "rationalized," that is, brought within limits, direction, and a form of control. By contrast, she argues, much social violence—especially male violence toward women—is irrational, lacking boundary and limits. Rubin and other lesbian-feminist defenders of sadomasochism have also stressed the point that sadomasochistic sex is *ritualized* and insist that it be limited by *mutual* consent.[37] (Parenthetically, we, not Benjamin, continue to believe that the lesbian-feminist sadomasochist thesis—that infliction of pain is acceptable between consenting adults as long as nobody gets *hurt*—reveals a certain confusion about pleasure and pain; but we do not suggest, nor does Benjamin, that practitioners of ritualized sadomasochistic sex necessarily suffer from greater confusion regarding the relationship of pain and pleasure or eros and power than do the rest of us schooled in patriarchy.)

Benjamin's analysis is promising at the outset because she begins by recognizing that Western culture's "individualistic emphasis on strict boundaries between the self and others promotes a sense of isolation and unreality" . . . making it "difficult to connect with others as living erotic beings, to feel erotically alive oneself." Initially, then, she identifies the source of disordered eroticism where a feminist analysis needs to locate it, in

> the increasing deprivation of nurturance and recognition in ordinary human intercourse. . . . The problem of domination begins with *the denial of dependency*. . . . The self that is strong enough to define itself not only through separateness but also through commonality with other subjects is able to recognize other subjects.[38]

Nevertheless, this insight does not lead Benjamin to challenge the peculiar notion of "self-possession" cultivated by patriarchal social relations. After acknowledging that denial of dependency is the key to domination, she then shifts to emphasizing the tension involved in autonomy.[39] "True differentiation," she claims, "means maintaining the *essential* tension of the *contradictory* impulses to assert the self and respect the other."[40] Benjamin needs a far greater appreciation of the *intrinsically* social character of selfhood and the irreplaceable character of community to human well-being. Surprisingly, she also misses the need for a clear break with the assumptions of psychoanalytic theory. Following Freud, she identifies eroticism with self/other tension. "True differentiation [is a tension] between negation and recognition." She speaks of "the tension of true differentiation and mutual recognition."[41] Even worse, she embraces George Bataille's extension of this self/other dialectic such that "eroticism *centers* around maintaining the life and death of the self."[42]

We have already insisted that it is easy in patriarchal culture to learn to experience eroticism this way. What must be denied, and denied categorically, in feminist theory is any assumption that this sort of eroticism is "necessary." As we have indicated, its "necessity" arises as a historical consequence of the twin dynamics of patriarchal sadomasochistic spirituality and capitalist patriarchal notions of self-possession. In both, antagonism and alienation between self and other are taken to be the expression of our "spiritual" or "natural" condition. Feminist theory must reject such claims to "inevitability."

It is not surprising that Benjamin's editors characterized her theory of eroticism as tinged with "Freudian pessimism."[43] If it is inevitable that our eroticism must be experienced as a conflict between life and death, or as a choice between self- and other-enhancement; if the best that can be hoped for is a delicate balancing of the warring desires for dependency and autonomy, there would be little reason to hope for a sensuous, eroticized culture. With Freud, we would have to acknowledge the social need for erotic repression, much as we might seek release from such repression through personal therapies.

Benjamin's work cries out for a far sharper break with patriarchal theory, if only to keep alive a feminist expectation that there can be relationships in which *dependence and autonomy are realized simultaneously through the erotic*. If we replace Benjamin's self/other relational assumptions with a thoroughgoing social theory of selfhood, as some religious feminists have done, we can reconceive self-possession and relations to others not as contradictions, but as a correlative possibility.[44] To do this, we must also relinquish the association of "autonomy" with "identity" and not speak, as Benjamin does, of "the autonomy of identity."[45] We are even doubtful of the value of the notion of "identity" in feminist theory. It is better, we submit, to think in terms of "self-integrity" and "other-integrity," such that we may simultaneously possess our own power, be empowered by others, and empower others. As rare as experiences of shared power are in this culture, it remains true that it is in those precious moments when isolation is broken that the possibility of community is grasped.

Nor should we continue to presume that the tension created by antagonistic self/other relations is the highest expression of sexual eroticism. If we do, the dilemmas of contemporary eroticism will surely defeat us. Tension is no more the inevitable hallmark of the erotic than it is an intrinsic characteristic of power. In spite of the pervasive connection between sexual excitement and interpersonal alienation that suffuses this culture, the goal of feminist ethics and politics is to affirm the possibility that eros—as body-mediated energy—can enhance mutuality and that deepening our sensuality will enable us to grasp the erotic character of all the relationships in which we are enmeshed. The goal is to *feel* our need for one another, to perceive human alienation as a violation of human possibility, a betrayal of who we can be. Benjamin is correct in saying that it is our incapacity to *feel* with others that manifests the crisis of eroticism we experience in a purportedly individualistic culture in which needs for dependency go largely unmet. But she has not unraveled the core of the dynamics that make existing eroticization so problematic.

Not surprisingly, Benjamin has interpreted the preoccupation with eros in our culture as a new religion or as a substitute for one. The religious "search for transcendence," she argues, expresses itself now through the erotic in the longing for recognition from another:

> Erotic masochism or submission expresses the same need for transcendence of self—the same flight from separation and discontinuity—formerly satisfied and expressed by religion.[46]

She is clear that sadomasochistic eroticism cannot provide an avenue to such transcendence. But she fails to recognize that she is also endorsing a patriarchal theory of religious transcendence and that there is a connection between this view of transcendence and a sadomasochistic patriarchal religion that desires absorption and is split off from embodiment. Such religion does not provide a living experience of transcendence. Benjamin rejects as misguided the intuition that the erotic is the key to transcendence.[47] By contrast, we believe *feminism ought to affirm an eroticism that grows from the soil of nonalienated relationship as a profound source of an experience of transcendence.*

PLEASURE AND TRANSCENDENCE

Transcendence, the wellspring of religious intuition and spiritual resourcefulness, is the power to cross over from self to other.[48] It is the act of making connections to one another, to the rest of creation, and, from a monotheistic religious perspective, to the source of our creative power in relation. Transcendence is also the resource of the desire to overcome structures of alienation such as heterosexism, sexism, racism, and class exploitation that impede even our best efforts to love our neighbors or ourselves very well. If sex is experienced as enhancing a shared sense of power, it is an avenue to transcendence, to deepening our relations with the world.

If self-other dynamics are fated to bear the mark of tension between self- and other-possession, then good sex can be at best an occasional, even accidental, striking of delicate balance. But experiences of good sex, however rare, precisely *lack* this quality of balance. The pleasure of sex is in its capacity to enhance sensuality; the full-body orgasm feels good because it increases a sense of well-being, of integrated bodily integrity. The pleasure in making love comes from experiencing one's own sensuous empowerment while being present to that of one's lover. Good sex involves a simultaneous enhancement of one's own and one's lover's well-being. Good sex does not involve simply one partner giving and the other receiving, one empowering and the other being empowered. The causes and effects of good sex are more complex, more dialectical, more interesting, and more difficult to categorize on the basis of separate roles or functions.

Insofar as sex is merely a balancing act, a matter of reducing tension, it is an alienated act which, while it may embody a desire to transcend alienated power in relation, can do no more than momentarily resolve it Experienced simply as an exchange of power or as a means of resolving emotional and physical friction in our relational lives, sex cannot move us beyond the zero-sum experience of personal power in which one person's gain is another's loss. As long as this remains our primary experience of sexual activity or desire, we are likely to be titillated by fantasies of being taken, ravished, or raped by those who hold power over us. Conversely, and less frequently among women in the dominant culture in the United States, our erotic images may be fueled by a desire to take, ravish, or rape those whom we wish to have power over or experience as powerless. We have tried to show that this sexual dynamic is a disturbing, often violent, embodiment of a broader social relation, and that this social relation lays bare the core of sadomasochism: *the embodied, sensual appropriation of absolute power, or abject powerlessness, in relation to others.* Our dominant culture and theological systems continue to legitimate this zero-sum power arrangement in which giving or enduring pain signifies good sex or good behavior. Whether we personally view this situation through moralistic, deterministic, hedonistic, or playful lenses, none of us as individuals, or as sex partners, can simply rise above the sadomasochism that deforms our common life.

We can re-vision, however, our life together in such a way that we participate in sparking a sexual *phantasie* that presses beyond sadomasochism. We borrow Dorothee Soelle's term to denote a reality that is more than simply "fantasy." *Phantasie* is generated by the collective power of human beings actively to "imagine" a present-future and, in so doing, to begin to create it among ourselves.[49] In our sexual *phantasie*, sex is fueled by the realization of ourselves as subjects of our own lives and as partners in the realization of common pleasures. In this sexual relating, which is political and spiritual as well, we realize our power as we are touched, delighted, and moved by others and experience them as subjects of their own lives rather than of ours. We discover that our pleasure is not largely in exchanging power or reducing tension but rather in realizing together the power that we have in relation to one another. Indeed, as Benjamin would suggest, erotic pleasure may always be enhanced to some degree by the tension between self and other. But our sexual *phantasie* is that the strongest and most durable pleasure has little to do with tension reduction between people who possess unequal quantities of power. It is rather a matter of relational celebration between people who realize sensually— in our bodies—that genuine personal power belongs to either only insofar as it belongs to both and who know deeply that sharing common goods, such as pleasure and self-esteem, generates more rather than less power and pleasure for all.

NOTES

1. Carol Vance, ed., *Pleasure and Danger: Exploring Female Sexuality* (Boston: Routledge & Kegan Paul, 1984); Ellen Willis, "Feminism, Moralism and Pornography," in *Powers of Desire: The Politics of Sexuality*, ed. Ann Snitow, Christine Stansell, and Sharon Thompson (New York: Monthly Review Press, 1983), 460–68; Varda Burstyn, ed. *Women Against Censorship* (Toronto: Douglas & McIntyre, 1984); Robin Linden, Darlene Pagano, et al., *Against Sado-masochism* (Oakland: Frog in the Well Press, 1982); Laura Lederer, ed., *Take Back the Night: Women on Pornography* (New York: William Morrow & Co., 1986); Andrea Dworkin, *Pornography: Men Possessing Women* (New York: A Perigee Book, 1979); *Coming to Power*, 2d ed., Samois Collective, a lesbian feminist S/M organization (Boston: Alyson Publications, 1982); "Sex Issue," *Heresies* 12, 3, no. 4 (1981); Haunani-Kay Trask, *Eros and Power: The Promise of Feminist Theory* (Philadelphia: University of Pennsylvania Press, 1986).

2. Mariana Valverde, *Sex, Power and Pleasure* (Toronto: Women's Press, 1985), 14.

3. Ibid., 9–46. See also Linda Gordon, *Woman's Body: Woman's Right. A Social History of Birth Control in America* (New York: Viking-Penguin, 1976); Adrienne Rich, *On Lies, Secrets and Silences: Selected Prose 1966–1978* (New York: W. W. Norton, 1979), 185–94, 199–202. For reviews of the development of literature on women's sexuality in the United States, see Introduction, in Snitow, ed., *Powers of Desire*.

4. Vance, ed., *Pleasure and Danger*; Linden et al., *Against Sado-Masochism*; Samois Collective, *Coming To Power*; Snitow et al., eds., *Powers of Desire*; Valverde, *Sex, Power and Pleasure*; "Sex Issue," *Heresies*.

5. Audre Lorde, "The Uses of the Erotic: The Erotic as Power," in *Sister Outsider* (Trumansburg, N.Y.: Crossing Press, 1984), 53–59.

6. Carter Heyward, *Our Passion for Justice: Images of Power, Sexuality and*

Liberation (New York: Pilgrim Press, 1984); Beverly W. Harrison, *Making the Connections: Essays in Feminist Social Ethics*, ed. Carol Robb (Boston: Beacon Press, 1985), 3–21, 81–173; idem, "Human Sexuality and Mutuality," in Judith L. Weidman, ed., *Christian Feminism: Visions of Humanity* (New York: Harper & Row, 1984), 141–57.

7. See the following essays in Vance, ed., *Pleasure and Danger*: Vance, "Towards a Politics of Sexuality," 1–27; Linda Gordon and Ellen Carol Dubois, "Seeking Ecstasy on the Battlefield: Danger and Pleasure in Nineteenth-century Thought," 31–49; and Alice Echols, "The Taming of the Id: Feminist Sexual Politics, 1968–1983," 50–72. See also Willis, "Feminism, Moralism, and Pornography" in Snitow et al., eds., *Powers of Desire*, 460–68.

8. From Vance, ed., *Pleasure and Danger*.

9. See Cherrie Moraga and Gloria Anzaldua, eds., *This Bridge Called My Back: Writings by Radical Women of Color* (Watertown, Mass.: Persephone Press, 1981); Cherrie Moraga, *Loving in the War Years* (Boston: South End Press, 1983); Rennie Simpson, "The Afro-American Female: The Historical Context of the Construction of Sexual Identity," in Snitow et al., eds., *Powers of Desire*, 229–35; Jacquelyn Dowd Hall, "The Mind That Burns in Each Body: Women, Rape, and Racial Violence," in Snitow et al., eds., *Powers of Desire*, 328–50; Barbara Omalade, "Hearts of Darkness," in Snitow et al., eds., *Powers of Desire*, 350–67; Bonnie Thornton Dill, "On the Hem of Life: Race, Class and the Prospects for Sisterhood," in Amy Swerdlow and Hanna Lessinger, eds., *Class, Race and Sex: The Dynamics of Control* (Boston: G. K. Hall, 1983), 173–88; Paula Giddings, *When and Where I Enter: The Impact of Black Women on Race and Sex in America* (New York: William Morrow, 1984), 84–94, 299–357; Bell Hooks, *Feminist Theory: From Margin to Center* (Boston: South End Press, 1984); Adrienne Rich, "Compulsory Heterosexuality and Lesbian Existence," in Snitow et al., eds., *Powers of Desire*, 177–205; and Joanna Ryan, "Psychoanalysis and Women Loving Women," in Sue Cartledge and Joanna Ryan, *Sex and Love: New Thoughts on Old Contradictions* (London: Women's Press, 1985), 196–209. See works by Linda Gordon, Mariana Valverde, and Carol Vance already cited; and Ellen Ross and Rayna Rapp, "Sex and Society: A Research Note from Social History and Anthropology," in Vance, ed., *Pleasure and Danger*. See also Rosalind Pollack Petchesky, *Abortion and Woman's Choice: The State, Sexuality, and Reproductive Freedom* (New York: Longmans, Green & Co., 1984); Beverly Wildung Harrison, *Our Right To Choose: Toward a New Ethic of Abortion* (Boston: Beacon Press, 1983); Rayna Rapp and Ellen Ross, "The Twenties' Backlash: Compulsory Heterosexuality, the Consumer Family, and the Waning of Feminism," in Swerdlow and Lessinger, eds., *Class, Race and Sex*, 93–107.

A few male writers provide extremely helpful historical-structural reinterpretation of the history of eroticism and confirm dynamics discussed here. E.g.,

Marco Mieli, *Homosexuality and Liberation: Elements of a Gay Critique* (London: Gay Men's Press, 1977). Mieli interprets male homosexual desire as universal and male heterosexual attraction to women as "split off," a form of hostility. He argues that so-called "heterosexual male sexuality" is always suffused with homosexuality. A British historian whose works are also important is Jeffrey Weeks, *Coming Out: Homosexual Politics in Britain from the 19th Century to the Present* (London: Quartet, 1977); idem, *Sex, Politics and Society: The Regulation of Sexuality Since 1800* (London: Longmans, Green & Co., 1981); and idem, *Sexuality and Its Discontents: Meanings, Myths and Modern Sexuality* (London: Routledge & Kegan Paul, 1985).

10. On mutual relation, see Carter Heyward, *The Redemption of God: A Theology of Mutual Relation* (Lanham, Md.: University Press of America, 1982); and idem, *Our Passion For Justice*, 83–93, 116–31. See also Harrison, "Human Sexuality and Mutuality," in Weidman, ed., *Christian Feminism*, 141–57.

11. Popular studies of women's sexual fantasies make clear that fantasies of seduction and domination are widespread and that even the repression of such sexual imagery may be understood as a response to domination.

12. Gordon, *Woman's Body: Woman's Right*; Valverde, *Sex, Power, and Pleasure*.

13. Margaret Miles has argued for this dialectical viewpoint in her study of Augustinian theology; see her *Fullness of Life: Historical Foundations for a New Asceticism* (Philadelphia: Westminster Press, 1981).

14. J. N. D. Kelley, *Early Christian Doctrine*, 2d ed. (New York: Harper & Brothers, 1960), 15–17, 127–37, 163–88, 459–79. Once the Neoplatonic dualism is presupposed, the dichotomy worked its way into Christian christological discussions. This discussion can be traced in Richard A. Norris, *The Christological Controversy* (Philadelphia: Fortress Press, 1980).

15. Elisabeth Schüssler Fiorenza has carefully reconstructed the repatriarchalizing process that occurred in early Christianity through the household codes; see her *In Memory of Her: A Feminist Theological Reconstruction of Christian Origins* (New York: Crossroad, 1983), esp. chap. 7.

16. John Boswell, *Christianity, Social Tolerance and Homosexuality: Gay People in Western Europe from the Beginning of the Christian Era to the Fourteenth Century* (Chicago: University of Chicago Press, 1980); and Bernadette J. Brooten, "Paul's View on the Nature of Women and Female Homoeroticism," in Clarissa Atkinson, Constance H. Buchanan, and Margaret A. Miles, eds., *Immaculate and Powerful* (Boston: Beacon Press, 1985), 61–87.

17. Samuel Laeuchli, *Power and Sexuality: The Emergence of Canon Law at the Synod of Elvira* (Philadelphia: Temple University Press, 1972), 56–113; Anne L. Barstow, *Married Priests and the Reforming Papacy: The Eleventh Century Debates* (Lewiston, N.Y.: Edwin Mellen Press, 1982); and Harrison, *Our Right to Choose*, 119–53.

18. Laeuchli, *Power and Sexuality*, 57–72, 102–13.

19. A few examples of this massive feminist research are: Rosemary Radford Ruether, *New Woman/New Earth: Sexist Ideologies and Human Liberation* (New York: Seabury Press, 1975); Schüssler Fiorenza, *In Memory of Her*; and idem, *Bread Not Stone: The Challenge of Feminist Biblical Interpretation* (Boston: Beacon Press, 1984); Phyllis Trible, *Texts of Terror: Literary-Feminist Readings of Biblical Narratives* (Philadelphia: Fortress Press, 1984); Rosemary Radford Ruether and Eleanor McLaughlin, eds., *Women of Spirit: Female Leadership in the Jewish and Christian Traditions* (New York: Simon & Schuster, 1979); Atkinson, Buchanan, and Miles, eds., *Immaculate and Powerful*; and Elizabeth A. Clark, *Jerome, Chrysostom, and Friends: Essays and Translations* (Lewiston, N.Y.: Edwin Mellen Press, 1979).

20. The theological significance of immediate relation is illumined in Heyward, *Redemption of God*, 2–9, and chap. 2. Heyward's discussion of "mutual relation" is indebted to the work of Jewish theologian Martin Buber. This work is also critical for understanding feminist theological claims that the effect of Christian dualism was to *denigrate* the human.

21. The tendency of men to separate "sex" and "intimacy" is widely acknowledged in the literature on sexuality. What is less frequently acknowledged is that this split reflects the social reality of sexist society: that men are to "desire" women sexually but are encouraged to locate equality in friendship—with men like themselves. Integration of sexual desire and intimate friendship remains a difficult task for men. We believe that Miele's analysis, *Homosexuality and Liberation*, explains not only why homoeroticism suffuses male sexuality but why so much male eroticism toward women depends upon women conforming to male tastes regarding proper femininity.

22. Samois Collective, *Coming to Power*. We note, in women's defense of sadomasochism, the characteristic claim that it is a way to come into one's power. Our uneasiness with this defense rests not in the fact that ritualized sadomasochism is too sexual but that its proponents tend to equate coming to power with personal *autonomy*. As we will argue below, such an equation incorporates a conception of power and relationship that extends the traditions of patriarchal social theory.

23. The importance of the Boston Women's Health Collective, *The New Our Bodies, Ourselves* (New York: Simon & Schuster, 1984) rests precisely in its stress on *teaching* bodily integrity to women. As such, it deserves the accolade "the bible" of the women's movement.

24. Susie Orbach, *Fat Is a Feminist Issue* (New York: Berkley Publisher, 1982); and idem, *Hunger Strike: The Anorexic's Struggle for Survival As a Metaphor for Our Age* (New York: W. W. Norton, 1986). See also Kim Chernin, *The Obsession: Reflections on the Tyranny of Slenderness* (New York: Harper & Row, 1982); and idem, *The Hungry Self: Women, Eating and Identity* (New York: Harper & Row, 1985).

25. The role of Christianity in anorexia is illumined in Leadoff M. Bell, *Holy Anorexia* (Chicago: University of Chicago Press, 1985). Orbach has illumined this thesis of female protest in her works.

26. Christian sexual ethics cannot fully transcend this spiritualizing tendency until or unless that ethic officially ceases to privilege lifelong marital sexuality as "the" proper normative form of sexuality. For a philosophical analysis of this problem see Dorothea Krook, *Three Traditions of Moral Thought* (Cambridge: Cambridge University Press, 1959), 333–47. A Christian ethic cannot celebrate sexuality as per se good because sex is only good when it functions to support other values—procreation, or, in liberal theology, "unitative" or "communicative" values. Even the most progressive Christian reinterpretations of sexuality tend to extend this spiritualizing tendency. When, for example, sexuality is affirmed because of its unitative and integrative functions, it is assumed that what sexual longing involved is the desire for *merging with another*. See Anthony Kosnick et al., *Human Sexuality: New Directions in American Catholic Thought* (New York: Paulist Press, 1977), 48–52. Charles Davis, a progressive who purports to affirm bodily sexuality in an unqualified way, nevertheless insists, "One yearns for the other as for a lost part of oneself, with a longing to merge oneself and one's life with the other into a single person and a single life," *Body as Spirit: The Nature of Religious Feeling* (New York: Seabury Press, 1976), 134. A Protestant example of the tendency to spiritualize love and evade sexuality is Frederick Sontag, *Love Beyond Pain: Mysticism Within Christianity* (New York: Paulist Press, 1977), 59ff.

27. It is interesting that there is a spate of recent bestsellers dealing with women's difficulties with heterosexual love and/or sexual relations. See Carol Cassell, *Swept Away. Why Women Confuse Love and Sex . . . And How They Can Have Both* (New York: Bantam Books, 1983); Robin Norwood, *Women Who Love Too Much* (New York: Pocket Books, 1986); Connell Cowan and Melvyn Kinder, *Smart Women: Foolish Choices* (New York: Crown Publisher, 1985); Christine Dowling, *The Cinderella Complex: Women's Hidden Fear of Independence* (New York: Summit Books, 1981). While several of these books are indeed helpful to women in disentangling their lives from destructive relationships with men, the latter two blame the victim and discourage women's relational expectations. What is more important to acknowledge is the *destructiveness of male socialization* that encourages fear of dependency. We also need a more rigorous critical perspective on female socialization in relation to the institution of compulsory heterosexuality than these works provide. See, e.g., Michelle Barrett and Mary MacIntosh, *The Anti-Social Family* (London: Verso Press, 1982).

28. Daniel Day Williams, *What Modern Day Theologians Are Saying*, rev. ed. (New York: Harper & Brothers, 1959), 135–37.

29. Harrison, *Our Right To Choose*, 67–90.

30. The classic formulation of pleasure as the central, and except for immunity from pain, the only good, is Jeremy Bentham's hedonistic utilitarianism. See Jeremy Bentham and John Stuart Mill, *The Utilitarians* (Garden City, N.Y.: Doubleday & Co., 1961), 100–125.

31. For an excellent analysis of the way male socialization conditions preoccupation with self-possession see John R. Wikse, *About Possession: The Self as Private Property* (University Park, Pa.: Pennsylvania State University Press, 1977).

32. This is probably the real source of the "difficulties" women have with sexual and intimacy relations discussed in the recent popular literature cited in n. 27. What troubles us is a tendency in feminist theory to encourage female independence, predicated upon a male model, rather than mutual relation as the simultaneous realization of self-possession and other-dependence.

33. The recognition that the experience of eroticized mutuality is so rare is one of the many insights that commends Mariana Valverde's analysis; see *Sex, Power and Pleasure*.

34. This theme of the eroticization of friendship is helpfully explored by Mary Hunt in *Fierce Tenderness: Toward a Feminist Theology of Friendship* (New York: Harper & Row, 1986).

35. Jessica Benjamin, "Master and Slave: The Fantasy of Erotic Domination," in Snitow et al., eds., *Powers of Desire*, 280–99.

36. Gayle Rubin, "Thinking Sex," *Pleasure and Danger*, ed. C. Vance, esp. 267–319, 303, 319 n. 75.

37. See Pat Califia, "Feminism and Sadomasochism," in *Co-Evolution Quarterly* 33 (Spring 1981). See also Nancy Wechsler, "Interview with Pat Califia and Gayle Rubin," Part I, *Gay Community News*, Book Review, July 18, 1981; Part II, *Gay Community News*, August 15, 1981.

38. Benjamin, "Master and Slave," 282–83. Emphasis added.

39. Ibid., 283–84.

40. Ibid., 284.

41. Ibid., 291, 297.

42. Ibid., 285. Emphasis added.

43. Editorial introduction in ibid., 280.

44. See, e.g., Ruth L. Smith, "Feminism and the Moral Subject," in Barbara Hilbert Andolsen, Christine Gudorf, and Mary Pellauer, eds., *Women's Consciousness; Women's Conscience* (Minneapolis: Winston Seabury, 1985), 235–80. See also Heyward, *Redemption of God*, 153–72.

45. Benjamin, "Master and Slave," in Snitow et al., eds., *Powers of Desire*, 282.

46. Ibid., 296.

47. Ibid., 281, 296.

48. Heyward, *Our Passion For Justice*, 243–47.

49. Dorothee Soelle, *Beyond Mere Obedience* (Minneapolis: Augsburg Press, 1970), 62–67.